HIP
HOTELS

FRANCE

HERBERT YPMA

HIP
HOTELS

FRANCE

with 538 illustrations, 387 in color

Thames & Hudson

introduction

I confess I am a Francophile. Not only that, I am a third-generation Francophile. My father spent all his student summers in France armed with nothing more than a bicycle, a tent and a slab of Camembert; my mother was an au pair in Paris. After a honeymoon largely courtesy of the generosity of French farmers and their paddocks, they have been back – *sans tente* – every year since. Before that, my grandfather used to make an annual pilgrimage to Val d'Isère for wintersports adventures back in the days when you still had to climb up before you could ski down.

Admittedly a lot has changed since then, but the appeal of France endures. The uniquely Gallic blend of nature, culture and food is difficult to resist. Not only does France have the highest mountains, the best beaches, the most enchanting villages and the most magnificent rivers in Europe, but it also has a rich culture in art, architecture, design and of course food that enhances these attractions all the more. In France you don't just admire the natural beauty, you truly enjoy it. Because chances are when you have finished a dip in the Atlantic or a day skiing in the Alps, you

will eat and sleep in a place that completes the experience of where you are. The cuisine and the culture of France intensify an already rewarding and varied travel experience. From the rugged coast of Brittany to the dramatic gorges and canyons of the Midi Pyrénées; from the green and castle-studded countryside of Burgundy to the sunburned Mediterranean landscape of Provence, the country is like a jigsaw puzzle of different pieces sharing a common language yet worlds apart in geography and culture.

That doesn't mean, however, that these experiences are easy to find. France too has its eyesores. Fast-food chains and spectacularly unattractive hypermarkets have sprung up all over, particularly on the outskirts of larger towns. But the romantic idyll that makes France such a travel magnet for the French as much as for foreigners has not perished; it has simply become more elusive. And that is the point of this book. It introduces a selection of outstanding hotel experiences that offer the France that we all want: the authentic France, the romantic France, the delicious France … the Francophile's France.

villa gallici

'When I'm in Aix I feel like I should be somewhere else and when I'm somewhere else I miss Aix … being born there is hopeless, nothing else in life will mean more.'

Cézanne was deeply attached to his home town of Aix-en-Provence. He returned here later in life, and was regularly to be found taking his daily apéritif at one of the many legendary cafés on the Cours Mirabeau, the town's main thoroughfare. The landscape of Aix, above all the Mont Sainte-Victoire, was the overwhelming inspiration of his paintings. To Cézanne, the light and colours of Provence, along with those of Italy and Greece, were the very source of great art. He dedicated his life to the quest to capture them on canvas.

Cézanne and his boyhood friend Émile Zola have become the town's most famous sons. Aix has certainly made the most of them. Every Saturday there is a guided tour called 'In the Footsteps of Cézanne' and on Tuesdays there's a Zola equivalent called 'A Literary Stroll'. Cézanne's atelier has been preserved as a museum, and no less than thirty-two locations in the city have been singled out as having played a role in the life of this enormously influential artist. The irony of all this adulation is that Aix didn't actually own a Cézanne painting until 1984, when the French state finally consigned a handful of small canvases to the Musée Granet.

Cézanne or no Cézanne, it's easy to see the attraction of this beautiful and refined town. It is blessed not just with a perfect light and climate but also with a far-reaching cultural pedigree. Medieval capital of Provence, Aix was established on the foundations a Roman settlement built by the conquering proconsul Sextius Calvinus. He called it Aquae Sextiae after the site's thermal springs (and himself, of course). Roman citizens came here for spa cures, an attraction that still draws tourists today: Picasso and Churchill both took the waters at the Thermes Sextius. After the Romans, the next great moulder of the city's character was the good King René. René was actually King of Anjou and in Provence he was little more than a count, but that didn't prevent him making Aix in the fifteenth century a great centre of Renaissance learning and the arts.

With its forty fountains and innumerable squares, trees and cafés, Aix is a place of aesthetic serenity, a quiet spot in the shade that is in every way the welcome antithesis of neighbouring Marseilles, with its hectic pace, frenetic noise and non-stop hustle and bustle.

All in all, the beauty, the peace, the colours, the light and the history make this town quite irresistible. No wonder then that Gil Dez, Charles Montemarco and Daniel Jouve were so persistent in their quest to persuade old Monsieur Gallici to sell his villa. They knew that this Italianate mansion, ideally situated in a park on the outskirts of the old town, would make a great hotel. Dez and his partners were focused on one idea – that of creating an authentic Aix experience, such as was no longer to be found in the city. They meant authentic in every respect – in architecture, design, and of course food.

The results of their perseverance are utterly convincing. Twenty-eight rooms and five suites, all completely different, but all resolutely Provençal in style. There are rooms with abundant white, rooms painted in bright southern colours, some cosy, some with lots of fabrics and some in the black and pistachio shades favoured by Christian Lacroix, also a son of the Midi. Most charming and most convincing of all is the ambience. It's as if they have taken the pleasure and atmosphere of a stroll down the Cours Mirabeau and transplanted it – water, trees and all – to the terrace of Villa Gallici.

For most of the year, this terrace serves as the lobby, breakfast room and dining room of the hotel. Traditional Provençal dishes are served under dappled sunlight beside the tinkling waters of an old fountain. At dinner both the tables and guests are a little more dressed up. A typical menu from Jean Marc Banzo, chef of Gallici's restaurant Le Clos de Violette, might include ravioli of *mousseuses* with a *jus* of truffles, or a *galinette* of fish in a bouillabaisse sauce, followed by a pear tart with a reduced wine sauce.

Villa Gallici has been described as 'all that is enjoyable about Italy presented in the best French manner'. On a warm summer's evening, as the elegant guests are wafted by the perfume of jasmine and the faint strains of the opera, it's not hard to understand why.

---

address Villa Gallici, Avenue de la Violette, 13100 Aix-en-Provence

telephone (33) 4 42 23 29 23   **fax** (33) 4 42 96 30 45

room rates from FF 1,500 (suites from FF 3,300)

nord pinus

Founded in the heart of Arles at the end of the nineteenth century, this hotel had its days of glory in the period after the second world war, when Nello Bessières, the famed tightrope-walking clown of the Medrano Circus, became the proprietor. He and his wife Germaine, an extrovert and extravagant former cabaret dancer, were determined this would not be another modest little provincial hotel. Together they set out to reinvent Nord Pinus as *the* place to stay in the Midi.

The hotel's *livre d'or* was signed in the fifties by everyone who was anyone. Christian Bérard, Paul Klee, Charles Trenet, Mistinguett, Louis Jouvet, Sacha Guitry, King Farouk and Yves Montand are just some of the big names that attended the flamboyant balls, parties and other occasions that were continually dreamed up by the Bessières. Nord Pinus became a byword for the worldly, the intellectual, and the artistic; and, this being the Camargue, the bullfighting centre of France, it also became a temple to *tauromachie*, the cult of the bull. For centuries Arles has lived according to the seasonal rhythms of the *ferias*, the festivals devoted to bullfighting. In the Camargue, unlike in Spain or other parts of France, the bullfight is not a fight to the death – at least not

for the animal. It is more often the *razeteurs* or runners, as they are known here, who get hurt. By tradition Germaine would always reserve room 10 for visiting heroes of the bullring.

Black-and-white vintage photographs throughout the hotel depict the matadors in their brilliant outfits and black capes, attesting to a period that for many locals was their city's finest hour. The legendary matador Luis-Miguel Dominguín, Picasso in his familiar blue-and-white *tricot*, and Cocteau, always the dandy, were often to be found together in the company of Germaine. After a fight Dominguín would appear on the balcony of room 10 to receive an ovation from the ecstatic crowd gathered in the Place de Forum below.

No party, however, can last forever. The death of Nello in 1969 left Germaine distraught. Overcome by grief, she lost interest in the hotel. Bit by bit the clientele, disillusioned by the disarray of rooms that were once so attractively kept, abandoned Nord Pinus. Things went from bad to worse. The restaurant silver was sold to pay the few employees who remained, and eventually, unavoidably, Nord Pinus went bankrupt. But Germaine refused to leave, and installed herself in one of the former guest rooms of the now deserted hotel.

Proprietor Anne Igou and photographer Peter Lindbergh live at Nord Pinus and are often found holding court in the bar

Picasso, Hemingway and Bogart adored the bullfights of Arles and the raffish glamour of the Nord Pinus

Echoes of Spain in a small shrine in the bar. The big-name matadors who visited here in the past were all Spanish

The walls are crammed with souvenirs of the days when this was a haven for bullfighters, celebrity artists and writers

A glass display case in the bar holds the ornately embroidered jackets of the legendary matadors

The food is rich in local Provençal traditions such as *soupe au pistou*, *brandade* and *clafoutis*

Anne Igou was a young doctor when she first dreamed of restoring Nord Pinus to its glamorous roots

Gingham tablecloths, red walls and poetic black-and-white photos define the highly unusual breakfast room

After the gregarious creator of the hotel died in 1961, his widow spent her days clinging forlornly to the banisters

Open from April to November, the hotel restaurant is a popular destination for dinner right in the centre of Arles

In tribute to Arles' strong association with the corrida, the walls are adorned with vintage bullfighting posters

Peter Knaup's photos capturing the balletic beauty of the bullfight adorn the blood-red walls of the breakfast room

Tiled floors, olive oil pots, chandeliers, dark wood, old leather: the style of Nord Pinus is one hundred per cent Latin

Tauromachie, the cult of the bull: for centuries Arles has lived by the rhythms of its biannual bullfighting festival

Nord Pinus is for those who like their hotels 'dark, seductive and haunted by history', as a visiting journalist put it

The renovated Nord Pinus retains all its original style, including details such as the wrought-iron bedheads

The ornate balustrade, Moroccan lanterns and giant candelabra create an exotic and oriental atmosphere

Berber rugs, African totems and other curios from the proprietor's travels sit alongside souvenirs from the hotel's past

Like a scene out of a Stephen King novel, she was to be found each day clinging to the wrought-iron balcony of the grand staircase, talking animatedly about the heyday of her creation. She almost never left the premises.

Continually pressed to sell, she eventually capitulated in 1987. The timing was tragic: Germaine died just days after finally moving out. The new proprietor of Nord Pinus was a young woman named Anne Igou, a doctor and native of the Camargue who became obsessed with the challenge of restoring Nord Pinus to its former glory. Whether in deference to Germaine's last wishes or out of respect for the hotel's illustrious past, she preserved intact the fittings and decorative details of Nord Pinus's interior – including the wrought-iron bedsteads that Germaine had commissioned from a local Arles craftsman – in the course of a thorough renovation of the property.

Anne Igou did a splendid and very well-judged job. She retained all those bits that make this hotel unique, but renewed all the features that contribute more to comfort and convenience than ambience or style. Thus the bathrooms, the plumbing, the telecommunications and the reception area are new; everything else is as it was. In the process she's also managed to restore the reputation. As a recent French magazine article vividly noted: 'amongst the *tauromachie* paraphernalia – the luminous outfits of past matadors, and the century-old posters advertising their *ferias* – it's the presence of people like Christian Lacroix and Ines de la Fressange that are testament to the fact that Nord Pinus has rediscovered its reputation for worldliness.'

The Nord Pinus is once again the number one address in Arles. The town too has revived its status of ancient metropolis with a new-found role as a cultural centre. International festivals of dance and photography are integral to the annual calendar here. And not only does the bullfighting continue, but room 10 is still reserved for those brave young men in tight pants.

address Nord Pinus, Place Forum, 13200 Arles

telephone (33) 4 90 93 44 44   **fax** (33) 4 90 93 34 00

room rates from FF 770 (suites from FF 1,700)

la mirande

For a period of almost seventy years in the fourteenth century, Rome was popeless. Instead the papacy resided in Avignon. Thanks to constant warring in the Italian papal states, Rome was deemed no longer safe for the leader of the Catholic Church, and thus between 1309 and 1376 Avignon was the seat of six successive popes, all French by birth: Clement V, John XXII, Benoît XII, Clement VI, Innocent VI and Urban V. The move was a financial disaster for Rome, and the city almost went bankrupt, but the installation of the papal court was a bonanza for Avignon. The population quickly increased to 40,000 inhabitants, making this one of the largest and most cosmopolitan cities in Europe. All over the city cardinals busied themselves building sumptuous palaces, each vying to outdo the last in pomp and ostentation. The popes, ensconced in the most magnificent palace of all, were officially awaiting the time when it was safe to return to Rome. But being French, they were apparently in no rush − and in any case, Italy was in a state of anarchic upheaval in these years. Eventually, in 1376, Gregory XI returned. For a while thereafter the Church was split between a pope in Rome supported by Italy, the Holy Roman Emperor, Flanders, and the king of England, and an antipope in Avignon supported by the kingdom of Naples, France and Spain. Eventually Rome won out, but the city of Avignon had forged forever its name in history.

The archives of the national library in Florence reveal that in 1308 the Cardinal de Pellegrue organized a reception in honour of his uncle Pope Clement V. The pope, his entourage, priests, cardinals and knights were treated to a huge banquet and a non-stop fountain of wine in an extravagant cardinal's palace in the heart of Avignon, decorated with huge tapestries. The entrance to the grand event was by way of a garden leading to the doors of what is now La Mirande.

That palace was destroyed by fire in 1411, but the house built on its charred foundations has survived to become La Mirande. Walking through its sumptuous and immaculately decorated spaces, it's not hard to visualize the splendours that the popes brought to this city. But in fact this impression of an extraordinary heritage is all a masterful illusion. When the property was purchased by the Stein family it was a depressing gothic mess. The facade designed in 1688 by Pierre Mignard, a brilliant court architect, was intact, but the interior had been destroyed by three centuries of bad taste.

Extraordinary attention to historic detail
was lavished on each and every room
of La Mirande

To achieve this degree of decorative
authenticity, wallpapers were washed
and wrung out before being hung

The stone staircase was modelled after
the entrance to the nearby Château
de Barbentane

Built on the site of a cardinal's palace that burned down in 1411, La Mirande is in the shadow of Avignon Cathedral

Besides this Louis XVI breakfast room, there is a Louis XV dining room, an Empire salon and a Chinoiserie library

The goal of the recent renovations was to create an interior that could be the product of generations of tasteful living

Achim Stein, a retired German engineer who made his fortune working on large-scale projects in the Middle East, and his wife Hannelore teamed up with François-Joseph Graf, a talented decorator from Paris. Passionate about art and antiques, they decided to renovate the property according to a hypothetical scenario: they pretended that Mignard, who had done such a fine job with the exterior, had gone on to design the interior. They then allowed for changes and additions by successive generations according to the ebb and flow of fashion – but this time all in *good* taste. That is how the new Mirande got its impressive library in the Chinoiserie style of Louis XV, a winter dining room in the light neoclassical style of Louis XVI, an atmospheric salon in the Belle Époque fashion of Napoleon III, and a formal dining room in the heavier baroque style of Louis XIV. But if nobody told you this was all new, you would never guess. The lengths the Steins were willing to go to create historical authenticity are astounding.

Handblocked wallpapers in the guestrooms were washed and crumpled before being hung; doors and windows were glazed with imperfect hand-blown glass; curtains throughout the hotel are lined with silk; and an impressive stone staircase was copied in extraordinarily convincing detail from the nearby Château de Barbentane. Wherever possible, salvaged materials were employed in preference to new. The result was neither cheap nor quick – far from it – but it is extraordinary, particularly for the ambience it has managed to create. Within these walls it is not too difficult to imagine yourself enjoying the privileged life of a seventeenth-century aristocrat.

Avignon today is still known as the papal city, and I can think of no more appropriate venue from which to explore this fascinating town. With a new TGV link completed, Avignon is now only two and a half hours by train from Paris. Perhaps in the future Avignon will be known not as the papal city but as the gateway to Provence.

---

address La Mirande, 4 place de la Mirande, 84000 Avignon

telephone (33) 4 90 85 93 93 **fax** (33) 4 90 86 26 85

room rates from FF 1,850 (suites from FF 3,700)

hôtel saint-james

Bordeaux is a big town – a surprisingly big town. If, like me, your associations of Bordeaux are limited to wine, then you will be taken aback by the scale and modernity of the city. It has a high-speed TGV connection to Paris, and its state-of-the-art airport is all high-tech gleaming glass and sculpted concrete.

The airport is an appropriate primer for the Hôtel Saint-James, which is not at all like the kind of houses depicted on French wine labels. The Saint-James is boldly modern, yet still perfectly in line with tradition: the French tradition of good food and hospitality, that is. Perched on top of a famous vine-clad mountain with expansive views of the bustling capital of Bordeaux below, the Saint-James is in the middle of Bouliac. This tiny village has a post office, a boulangerie and a church; it couldn't be more different from fast-moving, urban Bordeaux. It really is the picture-perfect little hamlet in the rural France of our imaginations.

The proprietor of the Saint-James, Jean-Marie Amat, is one of the superstar chefs of France. Regularly interviewed on TV, profiled in countless magazines, his name has become virtually a brand name. Along with Alain Ducasse, Michel Troisgros, Michel Guérard and Michel Bras, Amat is a trendsetter in French

cuisine, and the nation keeps regular tabs on all his latest innovations in the kitchen. In the case of the Saint-James, the restaurant came first. Set in a beautiful old stone mansion with sweeping views of Bordeaux in the distance, it was established to be a venue devoted to the perfectly orchestrated enjoyment of food. Rustic it may be, however, but it is certainly not remote – it is just close enough to Bordeaux to allow the city's residents to make the excursion quite comfortably. All the taxi drivers at the airport certainly knew of it without hesitation, which is a good sign.

Next came the accommodation. Amat held an architectural competition for a scheme that would provide a hotel as distinctive as the food and the setting. Problem was, nobody made the grade – not one entry excited Amat enough to dig into his pocket and take the plunge … until he met Jean Nouvel. The architect turned up at his restaurant, Amat immediately declared himself a big fan (particularly of Amat's famed Institut du Monde Arabe in Paris), the two sat down to lunch, and the controversial French super-architect got the job.

Nouvel opted for an abstract approach that reflects the qualities of the area: rugged and agricultural yet also stylish and refined.

Rural high-tech: between the pillows of the Saint-James guest rooms is a state-of-the-art Bang & Olufsen telephone

The corridor that runs past the kitchens is punctuated by a long thin window that gives a glimpse of the chefs at work

In contrast to Jean Nouvel's avant-garde addition, the dining room retains the features of an old mansion

The restaurant entrance gives little hint of the ultramodern architecture behind the remains of the original house

Architect Jean Nouvel, famous for his designs for the Institut du Monde Arabe in Paris, also designed the furniture

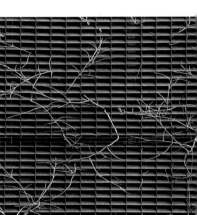

The steel grid that clads the exterior of the hotel was inspired by the utilitarian ingredients of rural working life

The grids change colour with the light and weather from orange to red to aubergine to copper to coal black

The pool is paved with anthracite-coloured tiles, creating a dark surface that highlights the reds of the buildings

More practical than a bedside table: a surface in the middle of the bed for the phone, and directed reading lights

High-tech hydraulics provide the necessary leverage to raise and lower the weighty steel window grilles

Operated by bedside remote controls, the grilles open out to the light and the dramatic view

The rooms at the Hôtel Saint-James are modern and minimal on the inside; rustic and tactile on the outside

The corridors of the hotel serve as a gallery, with work by a different artist installed every few months

In the private dining room of Jean-Marie Amat's restaurant the signature Nouvel chairs reappear in red

The light-weight, futuristic style of Nouvel's furniture suits the spare white interiors of the guest rooms

The radical architecture is right at home in the rustic surroundings of Bouliac, a tiny village just outside Bordeaux

The guest rooms are white, bright and minimal. Colour and detail come largely from the outside

Core ten steel, specially designed to rust, was used for the grilles of the Hôtel Saint-James

The cornerstone of the scheme is the steel grid with which he clad the exterior of the structure. It is reminiscent of the grids used by local farmers as livestock barriers, drainage grills and so on. As if that wasn't avant-garde enough, he gave it an added twist by making it a deep shade of terracotta rust. Except in this instance it's not just the *colour* of rust … it *is* rust. It makes use of a relatively new development called 'core ten' steel, which was deliberately designed to rust. The idea is that the surface rust then acts, like paint, to protect the steel underneath from further corrosion. At the Hôtel Saint-James, the visual drama of the red rust is intensified by the green creepers that intertwine with the grid.

It may all sound a bit brutal, but the grid cladding looks perfectly at ease in its rural environment. The interiors, however, also devised by Nouvel, are the polar opposite of brutal: white, blond and pristine, and totally devoid of nostalgia. The rooms are gleaming high-tech boxes designed to allow you to enjoy the surroundings – futuristic versions of orangeries, without the distractions of frilly Victorian rattan chairs or pot plants. The brochure describes the rooms as Zen; others call them minimal; but the struggle to attach the right label is irrelevant. What matters is that they work. You feel on top of the world: fully liberated and fully in control (no doubt partly thanks to the smart remote control that operates just about every item in the room). There is something profoundly uplifting about a place so unafraid to embrace the future.

Now back to the food. Jean-Marie Amat is featured in a book, available at the Saint-James reception, that profiles the brightest young stars of French cuisine and their signature dishes. For his contribution Amat chose *pigeon à la rose*, a dish that borrows from the cuisine of Morocco as well as the traditions of France. It makes a good symbol for the architecture and design of the Hôtel Saint-James … exotic, successfully experimental and supremely sophisticated.

---

address Hôtel Saint-James, 3 place Camille Hostein, 33270 Bouliac

telephone (33) 5 57 97 06 00   **fax** (33) 5 56 20 92 58

room rates from FF 900 (suites from FF 1,400)

fort de l'océan

It's a great name: La Côte Sauvage, the Wild Coast. But although it sounds dangerous, the only real threat at Fort de l'Océan is to your waistline. If you were on a ship, it would be a different story. This is the rugged and treacherous coast of Brittany, with thirty-foot tides, notorious storms and rocky outcrops everywhere. It's not a place for the fainthearted sailor. Even maritime professionals sometimes get it wrong, with catastrophic consequences. In late 1999 this coast suffered the terrible fate of an oil tanker running aground. Thankfully the damage was tackled immediately and on a vast scale. Now, just months later, only the odd black streak on projecting rocks betrays an incident that could so easily have been a full-scale ecological disaster.

No doubt the pollution was cleared so thoroughly because the area had so much to lose. This is a very popular stretch of coast: a picturesque, undulating expanse of rock formations lined with high-quality restaurants every half mile or so. As ever, popularity comes at a price. It's not always easy to escape the crowds. That is the appeal of Fort de l'Océan. This was originally a real fort with a moat, and it stands on its own promontory on a still relatively isolated stretch of the Côte Sauvage.

Built in the local granite that distinguishes the buildings of Brittany, it was converted to a residence in a later period, when the moat was filled in and another two floors were added in the same stone. Thus the small square fort became a small square château sticking out into its own little patch of the Atlantic.

By the time Louis Guérard and his wife came across it, the place was a ruin. The roof had caved in and the only inhabitants were the seagulls. As proprietors of three hotels on the same stretch of coast, they knew that they wanted to do something different with this property. It had to be an exclusive retreat. For this they entrusted the design to their Parisian friend Catherine Painvain. A stylist and designer of children's clothes, she is a regular holiday visitor to nearby Le Croisic. Her concept was simple. She had in mind a house not a hotel. Hence the nine bedrooms at Fort de l'Océan are filled with antiques from her favourite Parisian *antiquaire*, and no less than eight different prints and patterns were used in each room. The result is a cosy collection of rooms equally suited to winter and summer. Duvets are extra thick to allow the windows to be left open at night, the bathrooms feature the chiselled ceramic tiles originally developed for the Paris Metro, and the bed linen is real linen. It's the kind of decorative mix typical of comfortable old French houses.

The rest was left to the hotel expertise of the proprietors. Every conceivable detail, from the cuisine through to guest parking, has been thought out. The restaurant specializes in sea food and guests have the option of eating in the relatively formal dining room or on one of four separate and very private outdoor terraces overlooking the sea. Even the cars are housed in style. Hidden underneath the old fortified walls are eight individual garages that protect vehicles from the salty air and prevent them marring the splendid view. Judging from the number of guests dozing away in teak recliners perched on the rocks before the sweeping view of the Atlantic, many are happy just sleeping off lunch. Not that there is any shortage of things to do: for the golfing enthusiast there is a course just inland; in summer, the coast road carries more cycles than cars; for sailors the local marina is only five minutes away; and for

fishing you need only to clamber onto the rocks on which the fort is built.

This is an old-fashioned corner of France. People dress for dinner, and even at lunch time a T-shirt seems out of place. Until recently, most of the older women wore black and were rarely seen in public without the traditional Breton white lace capuchin. Bretons have traditionally been deeply religious, perhaps because their seafaring lives put them so much at the mercy of nature. Theirs is a region of stone villages, windmills and little old ladies who bake cakes. It's the exact opposite of the super-sophisticated sunbaked south: rugged, simple, old-fashioned – and less expensive.

Perhaps the way truly to appreciate the Côte Sauvage is to go La Baule first, one of the most commercial beaches of Brittany. After seeing this six-mile stretch of sand flanked by a four-lane highway and hundreds and hundreds of high-rise apartment buildings, the untouched beauty of the Côte Sauvage is irresistible.

address Fort de l'Océan, Pointe du Croisic, 44490 Le Croisic

telephone (33) 2 40 15 77 77   **fax** (33) 2 40 15 77 80

room rates from FF 900 (suites from FF 1,600)

château de bagnols

Château de Bagnols is not just a castle converted into a hotel – it's a slice of French history. From the tumultuous Middle Ages through the Renaissance to the glory years of the Bourbon kings and then the upheaval of the Revolution, there's not a period of the past eight hundred years that has not left its mark on this château nestled in the picturesque countryside of the Beaujolais Valley.

Through death, marriage and inheritance the estate changed hands many times. But it was always the residence of one wealthy Lyonnais family or another. Perhaps that's the key to its charm. It's grand, but still on a domestic scale. Like an old face that shows the evidence of an eventful life, Bagnols is filled with traces of the wars and famine, prosperity and tragedy it has witnessed over the years.

The first castle was built in the thirteenth century with a loan from the bishop of Lyons: the Church in those days was willing to swap financial support for protection. Lifestyle was a low priority in the original architecture; far more important was defence against marauding bands of ultra-violent mercenaries and bandits. The castle thus was not much more than a stone box surrounded by a dry moat and drawbridge. There were no windows – only slits just big enough to shoot an arrow through. Husbands waged war; wives stayed in dark halls to oversee the cooking and raise those children that survived the pestilence and violence that plagued the times.

As this part of France became more secure and prosperous, some domestic refinements were added. Tapestries were woven to provide adornment (and protection from draughts) and fresco paintings were commissioned. The Medicis, who established businesses in Lyons, brought with them the influences of the Italian Renaissance. The odd window was installed, but still the lion's share of architectural refinements were defensive. Special holes were made to allow the newly invented guns to be accommodated, while machicolation and stone buttressing created an overhang perfect for pouring hot oil on intrepid intruders.

The families under whose auspices the fort evolved over the centuries are too numerous and complex to list, but in general the function of the fort slowly changed from protective to domestic. By the eighteenth century, it had become an aristocratic estate dedicated to the enjoyment of life. Large windows were knocked through the five-foot-thick walls, and ceilings were raised and adorned with timber beams.

The west wall of the château, topped with machicolation, leads to the grove where breakfast is served in summer

Standing under the massive towering walls of the courtyard, one appreciates the building's military origins

Frescoes throughout the château are in the distinctive colours and style of this part of France

A detail of the old well reveals the medieval heritage of the thirteenth-century Château de Bagnols

Under a canopy of chestnut trees, this is the summer breakfast room, with a view over the entire valley

The medieval fireplace, renovated in the 1800s, is the original hearth of the great hall, now used as a dining room

The functional additions to the decor remind the visitor that until recently this was a working estate

Bathrooms differ in size and design, but all have sumptuous Napoleonic baths and lavish amounts of space

With a commanding view of the Beaujolais Valley, the grounds of the château are fringed by fragrant lavender

This being Burgundy, food plays a big role; the new head chef at Château de Bagnols trained under Michel Troisgros

In summer a canopy runs the length of the ramp leading to the dining room; the space is used for lunch and drinks

Deciding which frescoes to keep and which to peel away was one of the most stressful aspects of the renovation

A magnificent *lit à la polonaise* is the centrepiece of a suite distinguished by s combination of panelling and frescoes

The ornate stonework of the main portico was added during the Renaissance

The round pool is a recent addition. As the landscape matures it will be at the centre of a cherry grove

Centuries-old frescoes appear throughout the guest rooms and suites of the hotel

One of the most vivid of Château de Bagnols' surviving frescoes shows a typical eighteenth-century boar hunt

Much of the decor dates to a makeover in the late 1700s, when lifestyle at last began to take priority over defence

Fireplaces were installed to warm the spacious apartments, and luxurious fabrics and furniture were introduced. Despite the conversion to genteel life, however, the protective features of the building – crenellations, arrow slits, even the drawbridge – were preserved, for they were still symbols of status and power. Not surprisingly, they fell victim in 1789 to the Revolution: the crenellations on the castle's towers were destroyed in an act equivalent to punitive castration. The towers still stand, but their roofs slope off in a manner more like a grain silo than a military watchtower.

All this heritage was like a giant puzzle that Lord and Lady Hamlyn took on when they purchased the forlorn château in 1987. It was in a state of complete neglect and disrepair, but it was exactly what the couple was looking for. Lady Hamlyn embraced its challenges with such purpose and sensitivity that the finished result, which took more than four years to complete, earned her the title *Chevalier des Arts et des Lettres*.

In the process, numerous difficult decisions had to be taken. Some rooms had been decorated and redecorated many times over centuries, and the choice had to be made of which era to go back to – in particular, how many layers of fresco to remove in the likelihood of finding something better underneath. It was not a job for the fainthearted. This was a restoration on an industrial scale achieved with archaeological precision. Expensive and excruciatingly slow, the job was further complicated by the plan to make the place a luxury hotel. All the functional bits – smoke detectors, emergency exits, fire extinguishers, heating, plumbing and catering facilities – had to be allowed for without affecting the historic character. But the end result is not only inspiring, it's unique. Château de Bagnols is the only hotel in France that is classified as a *Monument Historique Classe*. It's a completely indulgent alternative to a history book – not that I don't like history books, but this is definitely better!

address Château de Bagnols, 69620 Bagnols

telephone (33) 4 74 71 40 00 **fax** (33) 4 74 71 40 49

room rates from FF 2,200 (suites from FF 5,500)

la maison troisgros

Would you get on a plane and fly for seven hours just to have a superb meal? If your answer is no, then you will probably never grasp the phenomenon of La Maison Troisgros. This is *the* Mecca for foodies. Troisgros is an institution in France, and indeed people come from all over the world to Roanne just to experience the food. La Maison Troisgros has had three Michelin stars for a record thirty-two consecutive years and counting. Michel Troisgros has cooked for events as prestigious as the G7 heads of state summit, and it is probably fair to say that every Frenchman who knows the difference between paté and *foie gras* dreams of eating just once in the hushed atmosphere of its legendary dining room.

Although the Troisgros family have now become a restaurant dynasty with five shops in Tokyo and a seat on the board of the prestigious Relais & Châteaux hotel chain, their beginnings were humble, like those of so many French culinary legends. La Maison Troisgros began in 1930 when Jean-Baptiste and Marie Troisgros moved to Roanne and set up a family restaurant in the old Hôtel des Platanes. The location was ideal in those days for taking advantage of the Paris–Lyons traffic. Grandpère Troisgros ran the place and Michel's

grandmother worked in the kitchen. But it was their two sons, Jean and Pierre, who really put Troisgros on the map. They inherited the family passion for cooking and after apprenticeships in such places as Maxine's in Paris, they returned to the kitchens of the family restaurant in Roanne, keen to make their own mark. By 1955, La Maison Troisgros had achieved its first Michelin star. In 1964 it was awarded a second, and four years later in 1968 a third, which through the family's consistent creativity and dedicated hard work it has kept ever since.

One of the two Troisgros brothers, Jean, died unexpectedly and suddenly in 1983. But Pierre carried on without him and in the late nineteen-eighties the baton passed in turn to his son, Michel. Apart from the obvious head-start of growing up with a father and uncle who were acknowledged as two of France's finest chefs, Michel added another layer to the family's culinary credentials by spending almost a decade working, learning and cooking with some of the most talented chefs in the world: Girardet in Lausanne, Taillevent in Paris, Chez Panisse in San Francisco and the Comptoir Gourmand in New York, to mention just a few.

These days hardly anyone drives any more between Paris and Lyons. The TGV is much faster and much more comfortable, but the reputation of Troisgros is such that people will journey to Roanne just for the food. And since after a memorable dinner the last thing you feel like doing is driving back to Lyons or wherever, the hotel was a logical extension of the Troisgros experience. Since taking the helm, Michel has placed his own personal stamp on La Maison Troisgros, not just in terms of what is served on the tables but also in the design and architecture of the adjacent hotel. Michel Troisgros is a keen fan of modern art and architecture, and over the past decade he and his wife Marie-Pierre have worked with some of the world's leading names in interior design to create a hotel that would be the perfect complement to the dining experience. Elegant, subtle and refined – like the cuisine – its design uses a palette of sophisticated neutrals and luxurious textures to conjure a thoroughly contemporary version of luxury.

It is the perfect retreat in which to contemplate (and digest) the incredible cuisine.

Just how good is Troisgros? The best way I know to answer that question is to tell the story of Peter Doucet. Doucet lives and works in Canada. He is a litigation lawyer by profession, not a chef, but his passion is fine food and cooking. At least four times a year he travels to the world's best restaurants not just to eat but to cook in their kitchens. His suit and briefcase are replaced by a white smock and chef's hat. He is undoubtedly one of the most serious amateur chefs in the world. As he says, 'I spend ninety per cent of my working life destroying things, so it's nice to spend the remaining ten per cent making things of great complexity and creativity.' On the morning that I was photographing the kitchen, he was on almond duty. For three long hours he first washed and then individually peeled fresh almonds, which were to be diced and finally minced. For what? To add a slight dash – a touch of *je ne sais quoi* – to the *foie gras*.

---

address La Maison Troisgros, 1 place Jean Troisgros, 42300 Roanne

telephone (33) 4 77 71 66 97 **fax** (33) 4 77 70 39 77

room rates from FF 950 (suites from FF 2,100)

le mas de peint

The Camargue is a triangle defined by the delta of the Rhône river. Its landscape, a protected national park, is a vast flat expanse where the sky and the sea meet in a composition of bold horizontal stripes. It's like no other part of France.

This is the land that Vincent van Gogh immortalized in his paintings. The flatness of the terrain no doubt reminded him of his native Holland. But he really came for the light and the colours, which are nothing like those of his country of birth. The Camargue is a small but distinctive part of France, a region defined by its white horses, its bulls and its flamingo-filled marshes. It is the French equivalent of the Wild West. The horse here is not a hobby, it is an essential part of the economy and the folklore. French cowboys who use horses to keep track of their livestock are still an integral part of the life. Fifty per cent of all the ranches in the Camargue are dedicated to raising horses and bulls, a fact reflected in the extraordinary number of local festivals dedicated to the bull. Legendary *gardiens* or herdsmen such as Jean Lafonte have made international reputations for themselves, so much so that they are considered more impresario than breeder, managing a bull's career as you might that of a

rock star. Not surprisingly, the culture of bullfighting is deeply entrenched, and the finest French bulls are bred here. So valuable are these animals that bullfighting in the Camargue is not *Death in the Afternoon*; instead the Camarguais invented their own form of the sport, in which the daring young *razeteur* makes a dash into the ring to pluck a rosette from the bull's horns, sprinting back to safety before he gets himself gored. Needless to say, in this version it is not the bull that is in the most danger.

Black bulls, white horses and cowboys decked out in the colourful indigenous Souleïado fabrics make the Camargue a Gypsy version of Marlborough country. And unlike so much of Europe, where traditions these days are often just staged for the tourists, here they are very much alive. Yet it's not always easy for the visitor to come into contact with them. The real Camargue is on the ranches outside Arles, and until recently, unless you had friends or family living there, you were unlikely to encounter it.

That is why Le Mas de Peint is so unique. Its proprietor, M. Jacques Bon, was born on the ranch and raised on his horse. Galloping through the muddy marshes to round up the cattle is as much part of his life as commuting to work is part of ours. He is a larger-than-life character with a huge white moustache who is never seen without a paisley shirt and a black cowboy hat. His seventeenth-century stone *manade* or ranch has been in the family for many generations. The decision to share his lifestyle came late in life. Just over ten years ago he and his second wife, architect Lucille Bon, opted to turn a wing of their property into a small luxury hotel.

Their plan was straightforward: to create an ambience in which guests could share the authentic Camargue experience. They would eat together in the kitchen among copper pots and antique armoires just like friends come over for a meal, sleep in simply furnished rooms, and be invited to go out on horseback to help rustle up the livestock. Guests were to muck in and share the life, not be pampered in the usual five-star fashion. There was to be no glitz at Le Mas de Peint, just genuine Camarguais hospitality.

But before you jump to conclusions about this being only for hardy outdoor types, don't forget that this is roughing it French style. The kitchen is the size of a small restaurant, and the chef, who turns out delicious Provençal fare, can only be fractionally short of a Michelin star. Lucille Bon introduced a distinctly urban edge to the design that makes this a surprisingly sophisticated retreat. The decor is artfully pared down, with a preference for neutral tones and natural fabrics. And while the bedrooms are simple and rustic, with exposed beams and brass beds, they are also sumptuously spacious. The bed linen (which is all linen) is embroidered with the brand of the ranch, and bathrooms are large and immaculate. All in all, Le Mas de Peint is significantly more luxurious than your average ranch.

So you can chase bulls through the marshes if you like, but equally you can opt to do nothing more adventurous than have a dip in the pool recently installed in one of the horse paddocks. The choice is entirely yours.

---

address Le Mas de Peint, Le Sambuc, 13200 Arles

telephone (33) 4 90 97 20 62 **fax** (33) 4 90 97 22 20

room rates from FF 1,195 (suites from FF 1,880)

maison du bassin

Cap Ferret? Isn't that in the south, down on the Côte d'Azur?

Even in France it's amazing the confusion you will encounter between Cap Ferret and Cap Ferrat. They're miles apart, and not just in distance. Cap Ferret is on the west coast, below Bordeaux and above Biarritz. Cap Ferrat is on a particularly popular – and expensive – stretch of the Riviera. Cap Ferret is laid-back, simple, unspoiled; Cap Ferrat is hyped, *mondain*, and anything but simple. Cap Ferret reminds me of the coast of New England: naturally spectacular and very popular with the 'boat shoes, chinos and polo shirt' set. It appeals to people looking for a back-to-nature style of escape. It's not a place for huge yachts and noisy speedboats; little boats of the sailing or fishing variety, preferably made of wood, are much more the order of the day on Cap Ferret.

Parisians, it seems, are deeply divided when it comes to holidays by the sea. Some are addicted to the heat and glamour of the Côte d'Azur, some swear by the charm and character of the Île de Ré, while others would not swap the raw, rugged beauty of Cap Ferret's Atlantic coast for anything. Topographically speaking, Cap Ferret is unquestionably the most spectacular of the three. Apart from miles and miles of untouched white sand beaches, it's famous for its sand dunes, said to be among the highest in the world. These mini-mountains of pale, rippling sand frame the entrance to the Bassin d'Arcachon, a large, well-protected, picturesque bay that was a favourite spot of Napoleon III and the Empress Eugénie.

Cap Ferret is a peninsula flanked on one side by the surf beaches of the Atlantic and on the other by the still, oyster-breeding waters of the Bassin d'Arcachon. This is a part of France defined by lighthouses, fishing boats and *tchanques* – beautiful cabana-like wooden houses built on stilts that were originally commissioned in the time of Napoleon to house the *gardiens* of the oyster beds (who prevented the populace of the region from simply helping themselves). Architecturally, the style of Cap Ferret has not progressed much beyond the traditional fisherman's shack, and most of the area's regulars hope it never will. Honest, unpretentious authenticity is Cap Ferret's most precious commodity, and people are prepared to pay for it. Despite a complete absence of châteaux, villas or other grand properties, prices are among the highest in France. Some of the country's most famous names have paid extraordinary sums for wooden shacks here.

But do not be misled: all this rugged simplicity is a bit of a smokescreen for the sophisticated lifestyle to be enjoyed in Cap Ferret. There is a vast choice of restaurants on the peninsula – some, like Sailfish, are nestled in the dunes, others, like Hortense, overlook the beaches of the bay. The seafood they specialize in is France's finest. But as it turns out, one of the best places to eat is also one of the best places to stay. Le Bistrot du Bassin, restaurant of La Maison du Bassin, is a local favourite, not just for lunch or dinner but also for breakfast. How much, you may ask, can you do with a baguette, some croissants and coffee? But have breakfast here and you'll see what a difference a truly excellent *boulanger* can make. From the freshly squeezed orange juice served in glasses etched with Napoleonic bees and the embroidered linen slipcover on the day's pastry basket, to the antique washbasins and French colonial furniture of the guest rooms, Cap Ferret's Maison du Bassin is one of those places that get everything exactly right.

Varnished wood, weathered leather furniture, painted timber, pictures of boats, white linen, model ships, pebbles, shutters, wicker baskets and the traditional light blue paint of beach-side cabanas add up to a decor that seems spontaneous and ingenuous. It's an impression the owners worked hard to achieve. The Paris-based couple were devoted holiday regulars in Cap Ferret and when the local hotel came on the market a few years ago they saw an opportunity to provide this exclusive little peninsula with its first truly *appropriate* hotel. Their ambition didn't go much beyond providing a nice place for their friends to stay – and that is exactly what they achieved. The staff are so friendly and the atmosphere so relaxed that it hardly feels like a hotel at all. In fact the only thing wrong with the place is the price. It's too cheap! At these rates the only thing that will save one of France's best-kept secrets from discovery is the faint hope that people will go on confusing Cap Ferret with its near-namesake on the Côte d'Azur.

address Maison du Bassin, 5 rue des Pionniers, 33970 Cap Ferret

telephone (33) 5 56 60 60 63   **fax** (33) 5 56 03 71 47

room rates from FF 500 (suites from FF 750)

champ des oiseaux

The proprietors of Champ des Oiseaux, Dominique and Monique Boisseau, have been working on their fifteenth-century town house for the past twenty years. Tucked away in the old quarter of Troyes, ancient capital of the Champagne district of France, theirs is one of those ravishingly charming hotels that no one will ever tell you about.

Historically, Troyes is one of the most important towns in the east of France. In the medieval period, under the counts of Champagne, it was famed for its great fairs, which brought the town exceptional prosperity. Henry V of England was recognized heir to the French throne by the Treaty of Troyes in 1420, and married Catherine of France here in the church of St-Jean-au-Marché. French Catholicism had a powerful base in Troyes and even today the squares surrounding the town's extraordinary profusion of churches fill up each week with devoted locals dressed in their Sunday best as they make their way to or from Mass – not something you're likely to witness in too many northern European cities these days.

Although not much of it has survived, the traditional architecture of this area is quite different from elsewhere in France. Without a good source of hard, stable stone (the local limestone is weak and porous), oak was used to give the houses their rigidity and strength. Massive beams arranged in cross-reinforced patterns resembling scaffolding give the original local architecture its distinct signature. The houses were traditionally finished in a lime render to which soft pastel shades were added. They make an attractive sight, sitting side by side in shades of pale blue, light pink and soft yellow, with their unique grids of external oak beams.

In 1524 a massive fire destroyed a thousand homes in Troyes. Because of their timber frames, most of the city's remaining medieval buildings have also been consumed by fire over the years. But miraculously a small corner of the old town remains almost completely intact. One cobblestone street in particular, situated just behind the cathedral, is a scene straight out of *The Three Musketeers*. It reveals not a trace of the past four centuries. Not surprisingly, this atmospheric quarter is a particular draw for visitors to the Champagne region.

Champ des Oiseaux is the only hotel in this historic area, and for good reason. This labour of love was never meant to be a hotel; it was created by the Boisseaus to be their home.

The architecture is medieval, but the bathrooms are bright, spacious and immaculately modern

The original cellars of Champs des Oiseaux were transformed into a surprisingly cosy salon

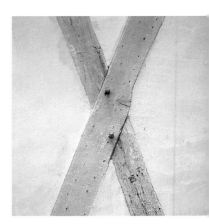

Absence of strong stone in the area dictated that buildings used oak beams cross-braced for structural strength

Situated in the heart of Troyes, the hotel is literally next door to the town's famous cathedral

The odd signature of the medieval carver's craft is to be found on the exterior beams of old Champagne

Modern conveniences, medieval architecture and bourgeois furniture define the Champs experience

As the project progressed, however, it gradually became clear that this medieval gem was going to be much too large for their own family – even their extended family. Thus, as is so often the story with the most individual hotels, they decided to turn it into a small, exclusive hotel.

It was, it seems, the right decision. Since day one, Champ des Oiseaux has been full or almost full. This success is not only thanks to its historic charms. When the decision was made to convert to a hotel, the same precision and attention to detail that went into the restoration were applied equally to all the features that make a quality hotel. The rooms retain their antique charm, for instance, but the *en suite* bathrooms are all, without exception, large, bright and modern in their plumbing and design. This place is all about the beauty of the old in combination with the convenience of the new – a tricky balance that the Boisseau family has managed to negotiate very successfully.

There's no restaurant on the premises (yet) but some of the best places to eat in Troyes are only around the corner. Breakfast is served in the old kitchen adjoining the original internal courtyard – a small cosy room with a big open fireplace for the winter. The hotel living room has been imaginatively created from the former cellars. It's a great spot for afternoon tea by a blazing fire.

After such a monumental effort, you might think that this family would now sit back and enjoy the spoils of all their toil and worry, but the Boisseaus have well and truly caught the renovation bug. The house next door is currently very dilapidated, but it has just as much potential. Thus they have recently begun the arduous process of extending their unique complex into this second medieval mansion. As word of Champ des Oiseaux spreads, they will be ready with more rooms for all those travellers who would welcome an escape into the world of Alexander Dumas for a few days.

---

address Champ des Oiseaux, 20 rue Linard Gonthier, 10000 Troyes

telephone (33) 3 25 80 58 50   **fax** (33) 3 25 80 98 34

room rates from FF 490 (suites from FF 950)

la colombe d'or

Picasso, Matisse, Calder and Delaunay all came here for the food, or so it is sometimes said. The famous Colombe d'Or *entrées* and the signature basket of salad were the attraction. Even when Matisse was ailing towards the end of his life, he would come in his chauffeur-driven Bentley to be served by Mme Roux in the back of the car. But my suspicion is that what they loved most was the artistic intelligence that is so strongly in evidence here.

The original proprietor, Paul Roux, had a true artist's attitude. In his later years he was encouraged by Picasso to start painting, and some of his work now hangs in the hotel. But you don't have to look too hard to find more general evidence of his sensibilities. For example the chairs on the famous terrace that serves as the summer dining room might look just like typical wooden Provençal farm chairs, but in fact they are *fer forgé*, wrought iron made to look like patinated wood. This is just the kind of twist so typical of an artist's way of thinking. The same is true of the bronze shells that illuminate the paintings in the dining room, the Eames-like bar tables and the rugged Noguchi-style stools.

It's true that the walls are covered with art that the world's top museums would kill for.

But Paul Roux's grandson François, who now oversees the day-to-day running of La Colombe d'Or, is not like other Picasso owners. He doesn't stop at each painting to pump you full of detail, nor is he particularly precious about these family jewels. The clear impression is that they are there to be enjoyed and appreciated, not revered. There's something quite wonderful about a giant Calder mobile perched on the edge of a simple but handsome swimming pool. This is how art should be – relaxed and accessible, lived with rather than viewed from a respectful distance with your hands clasped demurely behind your back.

There's an ease to the decor that belies the creativity that went into it. Just as Picasso could turn an old TV stand into a sculpture of a horse, the Roux family transformed a *maison de village* into an art-filled wonderland. It does help that the mountaintop village of St-Paul-de-Vence is one of the prettiest in the Côte d'Azure hinterland. But these days that can be more of a disadvantage than an advantage, particularly in summer, when the streets are full of sightseers no longer deterred by the long winding road up. Still, once inside this old mansion, the atmosphere is at once seductively avant-garde and reassuringly Provençal.

The hilltop village of St-Paul-de-Vence in the Côte d'Azure hinterland is one of the prettiest in the south of France

The massive proportions of the old architecture of La Colombe d'Or are complemented by modern art

A gigantic mural by Fernand Léger dominates the secluded leafy courtyard that serves as the summer dining room

While most of the hotel is eclectic and rustic, the bathrooms are pure function, simply tiled in local faience

A large mosaic by Braque framed by towering cypresses is the backdrop to the poolside recliners

Rustic and romantic: the bedrooms combine stone fireplaces, four-poster beds and old Persian rugs

The Roux family take the reputation of their restaurant very seriously. An army of classically clad waiters – black trousers, white shirts, black tie – prepare the tables and bring out dishes that were first served here more than half a century ago. Yet they started almost unimaginably modestly. Paul Roux, veteran of the first world war and son of a Provençal peasant, took on a small inn in St-Paul-de-Vence on his return from the front. The menu offered *hors d'oeuvres*, trout and chicken, and the sign read '*ici on loge à cheval, à pied ou en peinture*' (lodgings here for horses, pedestrians and artists). But by 1929 La Colombe d'Or had become the winter salon of international celebrities. To tell all the stories that took place on its legendary terrace would fill more than a few books. Even the abridged version of the legend of Colombe d'Or – the ubiquitous visitor's book – runs to seven volumes. Charlie Chaplin, Groucho Marx, Hubert de Givenchy, Winston Churchill, Jean Cocteau, Marlene Dietrich, Maria Callas, F. Scott Fitzgerald, David Niven, Rita Hayworth, Orson Welles, Cary Grant, Clark Gable, Alfred Hitchcock, Brigitte Bardot, Michael Caine, Robert de Niro, Madonna – the list goes on and on and on.

All the stars and all the art almost make one forget that architecturally this is quite a place – though what it was originally is almost impossible to tell. It's an eclectic arrangement of vaulted spaces, corridors, terraces and more terraces, all constructed in great slabs of rugged stone that give it a monastic quality. This stone was hauled here in three-hundred-odd lorry loads from a dilapidated château in Provence which Roux purchased and demolished for the purpose. It is said that when Roux died, Picasso was devastated, and his was one of the few funerals the artist ever attended. But for me the best example of the artistic attitude of La Colombe d'Or is the story of when King Leopold of Belgium came to stay. He had the nerve to announce to Paul Roux that he didn't like the paintings by Picasso, to which the owner replied: '*Monsieur, vous êtes un sauvage.*'

address La Colombe d'Or, Place du Général de Gaulle, 06570 St-Paul-de-Vence

telephone (33) 4 93 32 80 02 **fax** (33) 4 93 32 77 78

room rates from FF 1,500 (suites from FF 1,750)

royal riviera

The Riviera is the mother of all beach resorts. It's extraordinary to imagine that this small but famous stretch of the French Mediterranean is approaching its two-hundredth birthday as a fashionable retreat. Yet despite its colossal reputation, the Riviera is, geographically speaking, surprisingly diminutive. It starts in Cannes and ends in Menton, just forty-odd miles away.

The Riviera's original *raison d'être* was as a winter escape. Kings, princes, lords, barons and (later) industrialists came to the Côte d'Azur to avoid the rain and snow of the northern winter. It all started when Lord Brougham, former Lord Chancellor of England, was detained in Cannes en route to Italy in 1834. Charmed by the place, he built the Italianate Villa Eleanor, persuaded friends to join him, and proceeded to make the tiny fishing port fashionable. He succeeded beyond his wildest expectations. Maupassant observed here 'princes and princes – everywhere princes'. To feel at home, they built seaside palaces and employed battalions of domestics to keep the linen crisp and the lawns green. A vibrant social life, not a suntan, was in those days the main attraction. By the turn of the century, Cannes was like an annex of the most chichi areas of Paris.

The Riviera was already the height of chic, but the Jazz Age changed both the season that people visited and the clientele. Following the Great War, the newly liberated Europeans, desperate to shed the oppressive mantle of the old world, discovered all at once modern art, the Charleston, jazz, daring clothes and the suntan. To be *bien bronzé* was now something to aspire to. The new sun cult was artfully captured in the photos of Jacques-Henri Lartigue. The Riviera was no longer chiefly a winter resort, and the visitors were no longer all aristocratic. Artists (Picasso, Matisse, Cocteau) and writers (Fitzgerald, Hemingway) came for the sun, the food and the uninhibited lifestyle, as did the middle classes in increasing numbers. All in all, an enduring myth was established. The glamour, the money and the sheer beauty of this stretch of coastline made it the perfect backdrop for films starring Cary Grant, Grace Kelly and fabulous sports cars.

Although today's Riviera in no way resembles the original, it survives not just as a past legend but as a popular destination. So what has changed? For one the number of visitors. Cheap flights and an extensive network of autoroutes have made the Côte d'Azure very accessible – too accessible for some.

Abandoning the clutter of the Belle Époque, the Royal Riviera has been reinvented in a more Hellenistic style

With a superb chef, the hotel is also committed to reinventing the concept of hotel dining

Subtle combinations of terracotta, soft slate green, ochre and browns are true to the heritage of the Mediterranean

Inspired by the nearby Villa Kerylos, all the detailing, patterns, colours and shapes borrow from the Greek antique

The contemporary take on Hellenistic style gives this hotel a unique design signature

A sprinkling of colour and a strong sense of modernity define the new Royal Riviera

Nice is no longer a town, it's a cosmopolitan city. But there are benefits. Nice now has a showcase international airport, so a weekend in the Riviera is no longer the preserve of northern Europeans with private jets. Many visitors are very happy to take advantage of the proximity of a proper city: Rio and Sidney have profited from such a setup for decades. The large and spread-out nature of the existing architecture on certain stretches of the Riviera means they cannot fall victim to the dire fate of wall-to-wall apartment buildings suffered by Monte Carlo.

The Royal Riviera is a good example of the new upmarket approach. Another property in the stable of hotels managed by Grace Leo-Andrieu, it is an old gem reinvented for a new era. Today's Riviera client is no less demanding than a hundred years ago, but the expectations are different. Situated in the heart of the famous Cap Ferrat peninsula on one of the rare patches of green left on the Côte d'Azur, this grand old lady has been given a makeover that marks a complete break from the old Belle Époque style of the Riviera. Inspired by the famous Villa Kerylos, the new interior takes a neo-Hellenistic approach – that is to say, it marks a return to the authentic culture of the Mediterranean. The colours are olive green, umber, and sienna brown, and the patterns are simplifications of ancient Greek motifs. The point was to introduce contemporary simplicity without abandoning local appropriateness.

Perhaps even more important is the sophisticated approach to food. Once upon a time these hotels were renowned for their infamously anglicized menus. The culinary approach of the new Royal Riviera is urban and cosmopolitan. The five-star menu brings the ingredients of Provence to innovative dishes such as scallop hearts sautéed in olive oil, salad of baby squid, or small ravioli stuffed with *foie gras* on a bed of puréed peas. Thus in just under two centuries, the only real change is that the glamour has been brought up to date.

address Royal Riviera, 3 avenue Jean Monnet, 06230 St-Jean-Cap-Ferrat
telephone (33) 4 93 76 31 00   **fax** (33) 4 93 01 23 07
room rates from FF 1,200 (suites from FF 3,200)

hameau albert premier

Before World War II there were two main centres for winter sports in the Alps. One was the town of Morzine, and the other was Chamonix. The more spectacular of the two was always Chamonix. Located at the foot of the towering Mont Blanc, the highest peak in Europe, Chamonix is a Mecca for the world's best skiers, mountaineers and (these days) 'boarders'. Summer and winter alike, this old town fills up with eager young hotshots ready to test their skills on one of the world's best-known mountains.

The skiing here offers some of the steepest, longest and most challenging runs in the world. Chamonix has plenty of terrain for beginners and intermediates, but it tends in the main to attract the serious skiers. With these fanatics there are no late starts, no long lunches, and no 'shopping days because the sun isn't shining'. The town caters to a youthful, energetic and very *sportif* crowd who suit the Hameau Albert Premier perfectly – and vice versa.

Despite having the youngest attitude, this is actually one of the oldest hotels in Chamonix. It was founded in the early 1900s by the great grandfather of Pierre Carrier, the present proprietor, when the first railway line reached Chamonix. It acquired the name Albert Premier in 1920 in honour of the Belgian king, who was very fond of this town and a keen *alpiniste*. Pierre Carrier is a seventh-generation Chamoniard and, along with his wife Martine, an expert skier. On their odd afternoon off, they seize the opportunity to ski the type of vertical that most visitors would attempt only after a great deal of thinking, planning and praying – if at all.

Luckily for the guests this energetic couple take their work as seriously as they take their skiing. The Albert Premier is a member of the Relais & Châteaux group, and Pierre – who is the chef as well as the proprietor – has earned two Michelin stars. That's a commendable feat in itself, and even more so in a town better known for its skiing than for its food. But it's Maison Carrier, their most recent venture, that best reflects their unique approach to hospitality in Chamonix. Fashioned from the remains of fifteen farms, the oldest dating from 1794, this new addition to the Albert Premier combines the rugged simplicity and old timbers of an Alpine refuge with the distinctly colourful and totally unexpected modernity of design classics: pieces such as Le Corbusier red steel-framed *chaises* or a bright yellow 'felt' chair by wacky Italian designer Gaetano Pesce.

The towering peak of Mont Blanc,
Europe's highest mountain, is the
monumental guardian of Chamonix

The typical ceramics of the Haute Savoie
– very similar to the flame pottery of
Provence – decorate the public spaces

In traditional Alpine kitchens the bread
was put on suspended boards to cool
out of reach of rodents

A vintage twenties painting by Tamara
de Lempicka (a favourite of Madonna)
testifies to the long history of this resort

Besides Mont Blanc, Chamonix is also
close to the legendary Vallée Blanche
descent of the largest glacier in Europe

Some unexpected furniture provides
splashes of colour – in this case a chair
by Milanese designer Gaetano Pesce

An old grain larder sits in the reception
to the restaurant, beside the original
three-storey farmhouse chimney

Weathered beams, contemporary lamps
and Le Corbusier furniture combine to
create a youthful, sporty look

Mountain memorabilia decorates the
restaurant, which is itself an old
reconstructed Haute Savoie farmhouse

One small dining room, called the Gallery of Guides, is dedicated to famous nineteenth-century Alpine guides

Motifs such as cows and goats dominate the traditional Alpine craft of wood carving

One of four individual spaces in the Maison Carrier restaurant, this is next to the sloping wall of the old fireplace

Maison Carrier, the latest addition to the Hameau Albert Premier, is a reconstructed Savoie farmhouse

Old timber, antique Alpine furniture and the odd splash of bright colour define the interior

An old climber's rucksack in the dining room evokes Chamonix's historic status as Europe's premier ski resort

The bathrooms are gleamingly modern, executed in polished granite, stainless steel and green glass

Pure Haute Savoie tradition: weathered timber balconies decorated with the fretwork that typifies the region

Chamonix's winter sunsets, framed by Mont Blanc, are among the most sublime in the French Alps

These stylish intrusions are impossible to ignore, particularly against a backdrop of old beams, carved balconies and walls clad in massive half-logs. It's an unconventional approach to accommodation in the mountains, but one that suits Chamonix perfectly: sporty but luxurious. The rooms are large; bathrooms are spacious with state-of-the-art fixtures; and the carved wooden terraces offer a spectacular view of Mont Blanc.

For Pierre and Martine Carrier, Maison Carrier was a dream come true. But realizing their dream was an arduous task. For several years Pierre would get up at 5 am on his only day off to go in search of old farms that they could purchase, dismantle and reconstruct on the adjacent site. It was something the Carriers had been planning for some time, but they got really serious when they learned that the town council wanted to use the same site to build a municipal gymnasium.

Like its proprietors, Maison Carrier is both *sportif* and *gastronomique*. The Carriers used the opportunity of this addition to their existing hotel to also add a less formal *restaurant de pays* specializing in dishes of the region. It may not have the two Michelin stars of the Albert Premier, but the standard is such that I couldn't imagine a guest of Maison Carrier choosing to eat anywhere else. Faithful to the layout of an authentic Savoyard farmhouse, the restaurant is arranged around a massive three-storey chimney. This traditional wood-burning smokestack is used to cure meats and sausages. The various dining rooms that surround its imposing structure vary in size and shape, but they share an authentic Alpine approach to the decoration. The details are all inspired by the location. Old rucksacks, weathered pickaxes, oil paintings of the peak, and ancient sepia photographs of legendary Alpine guides are evocative reminders of the majesty and challenge of Chamonix's mountains. If anyone ever does a remake of Clint Eastwood's *The Eiger Sanction*, a tough, gritty thriller set in the Alps, this would be the perfect location.

---

address Hameau Albert Premier, 119 impasse du Montenvers, 74402 Chamonix
telephone (33) 4 50 53 05 09   **fax** (33) 4 50 55 95 48
room rates from FF 760 (suites from FF 1,500)

hôtel mont blanc

Just as the Parisians are split into definite camps in their preference for seaside resorts, so they are quite passionate about their choice of winter playground. They can be very territorial in their defence of their own favourites and utterly dismissive of everywhere else. Courchevel, they will tell you, is for the *nouveau riche*; Val d'Isère has too many English tourists; Avoriaz too many Dutch; while Megève is for people who would rather walk around in fur coats than ski.

As usual, there's an element of truth in all these generalizations: Val d'Isère *is* very popular with the English; there *are* an awful lot of Dutch skiers in Avoriaz; and they *do* wear a lot of fur coats in Megève. But beyond all that is the basic truth that these resorts are very different, and that's precisely what makes the French Alps so attractive: the variety and the choice. In a sense it's futile to compare these places with one another – it's like comparing apples with oranges.

Megève does offer probably the least challenging skiing of all the better known French resorts, but to dismiss it for that is to miss the point. For skiing in Megève is also about enjoying the charm, authenticity and lifestyle of the Haute Savoie's prettiest village.

For starters, any little goat shed on Megève's mountains is likely to serve better food and offer a better wine list than the most expensive restaurants of other resorts. There are fewer snack bars, fast-food outlets or self-service cafeterias on the slopes of Megève than anywhere in the French Alps. The local council has always been very strict about enforcing building codes and preserving the local style, with the result that there are also fewer eyesores. The *art de vivre* here is about integrating some skiing into all the other activities and facilities the town has to offer – not the other way around.

With its beautiful shops and its Michelin-starred restaurants (Marc Veyrat's has three), Megève is a little town as sophisticated as the crowd it has always drawn. And traditionally this crowd would meet at the Hotel Mont Blanc. One of the oldest and most central hotels in Megève, the Mont Blanc's greatest period was after the war and George Boisson's renovation of 1949, when Megève became 'the 21st arrondissement of Paris', as Jean Cocteau memorably rebaptised it. Here you were as likely to run into Audrey Hepburn, Hubert de Givenchy, Charles Aznavour, Roger Vadim or Rita Hayworth as François Mitterand. Cocteau even created a series of murals to decorate many of the rooms.

The Mont Blanc retained this high profile until the early seventies, when the fashion, and the crowd, shifted to the newer, bigger resorts. They were higher, they had more snow and their lifts were significantly quicker. 'Linked terrain' became the new buzzword as a leap in technology ushered in a new era of skiing. The purpose-built resorts of Les Trois Vallées, Tignes, Val d'Isère and Les Portes du Soleil made it possible to ski from one village to another via an extensive network of high-speed lifts. This catapulted them into the front rank. Megève too eventually updated its lifts and established extensive links with neighbouring mountains such as St-Gervais, but it could never hope to compete with the greater altitude and capacity of the super resorts. So instead Megève opted to specialize in the area in which it already led the field, namely lifestyle.

By discouraging package tours, prohibiting large hotel developments or apartment blocks, and investing in authenticity and quality, the town chose the direction of 'small but beautiful'. This choice has paid off very well, particularly in the last decade. The celebrities are back, property prices are booming, and the town is almost always booked out. And, perhaps not surprisingly, Jean-Louis and Jocelyne Sibuet stepped in with their hugely successful Compagnie des Montagnes to take over the Hôtel Mont Blanc.

The Sibuets gave the place a total makeover while managing to preserve perfectly the ambience of this long-established mountain hotel. The style of the new Mont Blanc interior, in keeping with its stellar past, is more sophisticated than the Sibuets' other hotels. The pine panelling that extends throughout the lobby, lounge, dining room and most of the guest rooms, for example, is of a style that owes its origins more to a château than a refuge. It's still Savoyard, but this time 'more mansion, less farmhouse'. And, needless to say, they kept the Cocteau murals.

address Hôtel Mont Blanc, Place de l'Église, 74120 Megève

telephone (33) 4 50 21 20 02   **fax** (33) 4 50 21 45 28

room rates from FF 850 (suites from FF 1,390)

le lodge park

The renovation of the traditional Grand Hotel du Parc, located in the very heart of Megève, gave Jean-Louis and Jocelyne Sibuet their first opportunity to try out other formulas for holidays in the snow after their great success with Fermes de Marie (p. 103).

They completed the work in Christmas 1996. Le Lodge Park is totally different from their other hotels. Its visual inspiration was the spirit of adventure. Fishing, hunting and mountaineering provide the decorative themes. The result has more in common with a lodge in America than a chalet in the Haute Savoie. In fact the entire hotel could pass for the set of a Ralph Lauren sportswear advert: natural river stone, weathered timber, aged leather and Scottish plaid set the tone. From the bar to the restaurant to the rooms, the ambience is that of a log-cabin camp in the Adirondacks. This themed approach has worked like a charm, attracting a youthful, sporty crowd to Megève. By ten in the morning there is no one left in the hotel apart from the staff. And contrary to Megève's reputation as a non-skiing resort, they are all out on the slopes.

As with Fermes de Marie, the Sibuets have ensured that Le Lodge Park is completely self-contained, with every luxury and necessity laid on. A small pro-shop fulfils any equipment needs, there is a well-equipped spa and health centre, and the hotel is instrumental in organizing excursions that take you beyond the usual boundaries of the resort.

One of the best adventures, reserved exclusively for the guests of a Sibuet hotel, is an excursion to the mountain refuge that they also own and operate. The best way to get there is to ski. It helps to have a map (which reception can provide), but the basic route is simple enough – up, down, up down, working your way across the mountain by a series of different lifts until you reach a particular remote peak. Behind it lies a valley untouched by modern ski development. It's like the lost valley of Shangri-la – no lifts and no buildings. Your destination, a wooden shack in the valley, is hidden from the pistes by a long, thick ridge of pine trees. The final descent to the refuge is an adventure on its own. A steep winding trail with a giddying ravine on one side provides plenty of heart-stopping drama.

It's worth every ounce of adrenalin. This is the stuff of legend – a real Hemingway fantasy in a setting like something out of *Seven Years in Tibet*, a steep snow-covered valley plunging into a funnel shape below the refuge.

Le Lodge Park is situated in Megève, easily the prettiest little village in the Haute Savoie

American hunting lodge chic with a French twist: the style of Le Lodge Park is quite unique

Stairs from the ground-floor lobby lead up to the in-house pro-shop, beauty clinic, health spa and conference area

Breakfast cereals are served in muslin bags: presentation plays a big role in the Lodge Park experience

Lots of antlers and a sprinkling of exoticism: the groovy ambience attracts a youthful and sporty crowd

Brightly coloured Scottish plaids against massive wooden beams make the log-cabin-style bedrooms warm and inviting

The fireplace on the ground floor, made from river stone and birch logs, takes up an entire corner of the lobby

Infinite attention to detail is the hallmark of the Sibuets' approach to hotel-keeping

The downstairs 'Atelier du Ski' is a small rental boutique stocked with all the latest equipment

helves made from silver birch are used to display a colourful collection of fruits and pulses

Ralph Lauren in the French Alps: the distinctive plaids complement the rugged furnishings and eclectic decor

The lower ground floor houses extensive post-ski recovery facilities, including saunas, plunge pools and jacuzzi

Antlers and more antlers, fishing rods and outdoor paraphernalia mark this t as the sportiest of the Sibuets' hotels

Shooting, fishing, mountaineering: the look is American, but the traditions are no less French

Bedrooms are cosy and chunky, with bedside walls formed of huge exposed logs

The outstanding cuisine at Le Lodge Park was recently awarded a Michelin star

Vintage skiing photos, beaten-up leather club chairs, big logs, and lots and lots of antlers define the decor here

The spa specializes in beauty treatments with an Alpine twist should you feel in need of some post-ski pampering

A pine forest directly above the refuge is protected from the elements by a massive granite ridge that hangs ominously over the whole area. It's a spectacular site for a spectacular shack. Nowhere else in the Alps will you find a refuge like it. This is as authentic as it gets – no heating, no bathrooms, no modern technology (if you excuse a little electricity). The Sibuets resisted all temptation to tart the place up. It's exactly as it would have been more than a century ago, when local farmers built these refuges in the summer in case they and their cattle were cut off by early snows in the winter. It is surprisingly large, with an enormous two-storey stone fireplace as a centrepiece and plenty of space to feed a crowd of hungry ski-adventurers. It wouldn't be a Sibuet experience if the culinary part of the equation was not done to perfection. Every morning the staff leave early on their skis to get to the old wooden house in time to prepare for the day's guests. By the time the first flush-faced adventurer comes barrelling down the final trail, the meats, the cheeses, the breads, the soups and the boysenberry tarts that are all part of a traditional Savoyard mountain lunch are ready. On warm sunny days this is served outside on a long wooden table overlooking the valley. On cold blustery days you eat inside with a big fire blazing in the hearth.

The truly adventurous can choose to stay overnight in the small rustic rooms upstairs. With not much more in the way of shelter than timber floors, timber walls and thick eiderdowns (no heating, remember), most opt for a lift back up in the Sibuets' snow cat. With great hoots of laughter (helped by the pre- and post-lunch schnapps), they are hitched up to one giant tow rope and pulled like water-skiers – en masse – back up that treacherous little trail to the other side of the pine-covered ridge, whereupon everyone is set free to ski their way back down to the village. A day at the Sibuet refuge will make you feel like Sir Edmund Hillary – even if you ski like Eddie the Eagle.

address Le Lodge Park, 100 rue d'Arly, 74120 Megève

telephone (33) 4 50 93 05 03 **fax** (33) 4 50 93 09 52

room rates from FF 990 (suites from FF 2,780)

les fermes de marie

Who would have imagined while Jean-Louis Sibuet was busy salvaging, dismantling and reconstructing old goat sheds, mountain huts, barns, sheep stalls, stables and derelict farms in the Haute Savoie twenty years ago what a trend he and his wife Jocelyne were to set in the business of hospitality in the snow?

They originally started to build from their assemblage of architectural bits and pieces without any idea of what the final result would look like, as they freely admit. All they knew was that it was to be in the true spirit of a Savoyard farm. While her husband was busy with the reconstructions – trying to make sense of huge collections of numbered beams and labelled planks – Jocelyne, a passionate fan of decoration, immersed herself in the cultural detail of the Haute Savoie, the region of France that includes the highest peaks of the Alps. Authentic regional furniture, local ceramics, even traditional carved butter moulds – anything and everything that is part of the visual ingredients of the Haute Savoie became her passion. The plates, the cutlery, the furniture and the fabrics were all meticulously researched in an effort to recreate the intimacy and character of a traditional farmhouse. If it no longer existed, she found someone to make it again, and in the process became an enthusiastic patron of the ateliers of the region.

The rest, as they say, is history. The Sibuets succeeded way beyond their own and anybody else's expectations; certainly, they achieved far more than merely to establish a successful hotel. Since the opening of Les Fermes de Marie in 1989, 'old timber' and 'Savoyard farmhouse' have become the buzzwords of the industry. Suddenly every old house on the market in the snow is referred to by real estate agents as a 'farm' and style magazines have become obsessed with 'rustic with a twist' interiors. And as a more permanent indicator of the trend, a host of coffee-table books has emerged dedicated to this same Alpine style.

In the meantime, the eight chalets of Les Fermes de Marie have become an institution. This 'village of Savoyard style in the very heart of Megève', as the magazines describe it, has all but stolen the charm and character initiative from the Austrians. Until the Sibuets launched their version of *le style savoyard* it was generally acknowledged that while France had better skiing, Austria was more *gemütlich*. French mountains were higher, bigger and steeper, but Austrian hotels were cosier and prettier. Fermes de Marie changed all that.

Old timbers rescued from dilapidated mountain shacks give Les Fermes de Marie warmth and character

Breakfast and afternoon tea are served in these vaulted spaces decorated with Alpine frescoes

Guests in need of transportation can choose between Land Rover or horse-drawn sled

One of the hotel's most exquisite features is the indoor pool set in the shell of an old mountain *bergerie*

The terrace alongside the traditional fondue restaurant is a popular setting for lunch on sunny days

Many of the guest rooms are more like small mountain huts, complete with fireplace (and mod cons)

With its interior of rugged weather-worn timber beams, red gingham fabrics, simple wooden chairs, traditional handmade pottery, rustic panelled walls and roaring fires, the Sibuets created an embodiment of the romantic ideal of a chalet in the snow. Clichéd? Maybe. But no more so than the gingerbread houses of Austria. Fermes de Marie is like a French Tirol minus the *lederhosen*, though for my money the Sibuets have the edge over their yodelling neighbours. This is France after all, and the food at Fermes de Marie is as convincing as the ambience. There are no less than three restaurants here, one of them located in an enormous barn-like space that – naturally – was once a barn. Under beams adorned with antique cow bells and oil paintings of Savoyard ancestors, skiers and non-skiers enjoy a level of cuisine normally exclusive to upmarket city restaurants. For variety there is also a cheese restaurant adjacent to a terrace that offers an ideal lunchtime venue on blue-sky days.

Total indulgence is the name of the game at Les Fermes de Marie. It's difficult to think of anything the Sibuets left out in their determination to pamper their guests into submission. The indoor swimming pool built into yet another rescued old *bergerie* has a spectacular view over the surrounding mountains, the gym is equipped with state-of-the-art cardio fitness equipment, the beauty centre caters to every cosmetic whim you could dream up for skin, hair or muscles (with an entire array of their own mountain cosmetics), the vaulted spaces of the breakfast room are also an ideal venue for afternoon tea and cake, and there are upstairs spaces under the massive beams perfect for curling up by a fire with a book. Even the cars are catered to by a large heated underground parking gallery. The Sibuets have invented a new kind of skiing that is all indulgence and no hardship – where the thought of venturing out into the cold is quite probably the nearest you will get to the slopes all day.

address Les Fermes de Marie, Chemin de Riante Colline, 74120 Megève
telephone (33) 4 50 93 03 10 **fax** (33) 4 50 93 09 84
room rates from FF 1,050 (suites from FF 1,670)

le mas de la coutettaz

As a skiing destination the French Alps have in some ways become a victim of their own success. Super ski resorts like Tignes-Val d'Isère may offer extraordinary sporting possibilities, but they have fallen victim to the woeful mediocrity that invariably overtakes resort architecture and design. Tignes in particular is just plain ugly: nothing but towering concrete blocks built in the days when expansion was the only priority, and environmental or aesthetic impact simply not on the agenda.

Now France is stuck with them. Not only have these apartment complexes aged badly, but – worse – given a choice, most skiers would far rather opt for the charm and character of a real Alpine village. Unfortunately France has an ever dwindling number of these. This is what makes Mas de la Coutettaz so unusual and so special. Not only is it located smack in the middle of Morzine, one of the original Haute Savoie wintersports villages, but it has survived to this day as a real farmhouse without ever being modernized, renovated, or dismantled and moved to another location. It has never been a restaurant, bar or ski shop. Until very recently it was a house, and it hasn't lost any of its domestic features – which is precisely what makes it a great hotel.

In a recent survey, a French magazine voted Morzine the Alpine destination most likely to surprise – that is, to provide something unexpected. Morzine, you see, is still a real town. The local slate mines brought prosperity here long before the ski bug hit the mountains. (Slate was traditionally used for roofing in Alpine regions.) And even when the ski boom did take off, the town didn't become a slave to tourism, thanks to a new complex – Avoriaz – which was built nearby to accommodate the visitors. Thus Morzine remained intact as a town. It does have the odd hotel, but only for those guests prepared to make the journey each day to Avoriaz for their skiing.

All this explains why such an impressive and imposing house in the middle of town could have gone relatively unnoticed. Built in the eighteenth century by the owner of a slate mine – the origin of his wealth is evidenced in the enormous slabs of slate used throughout the ground floor – this manor house is the oldest building in the valley. It had been on the market for quite some time when Dorrien Ricardo, an English expat who first discovered the unspoiled charms of Morzine while working for a tour operator in the area, plucked up the courage to make a bid.

Morzine, along with Chamonix,
is one of the original wintersports
centres of the French Alps

The quality of the building can be
discerned from the solid granite door
frames and carved wooden doors

Bathrooms (each room has one) and
heating were the only modernizations
conceded in this rustic farmhouse

as de la Coutettaz is surrounded by the pistes of one of the largest linked ski fields in Europe

Beautifully detailed woodwork reveals a farmhouse built on the fat profits of the region's slate mining

Some of the rooms retain their original fireplaces installed by the first proprietor

By unfortunate chance, at the very same moment the town council announced plans to turn the house into a local library. A long battle ensued, but eventually Dorrien was allowed to go ahead with his dream of converting the farmhouse into a small hotel – provided he didn't alter any of the original features. As it turned out, he didn't have the budget to do anything more than update the plumbing and heating and install a commercial kitchen. In retrospect this restraint was perfectly appropriate, since it left intact all the ancient Savoyard character and ambience of the property.

The Coutettaz experience is what Alpine skiing must have been about before the hotel chains and property developers tried their damnedest to ruin it. Perhaps it's because each night all the guests eat together at a single giant candlelit table set up in the former stables. Dinner (and breakfast) is included in the room rate. The style of the food is very farmhouse – lots of noise and lots to eat (more than anyone can manage). The ambience is a cross between a university college dining room, a German beer festival and an evening with the Waltons. Even if you don't know anyone (as I didn't) you soon will, because that's what inevitably happens when you sit at a table with twenty-odd people. It's not sophisticated, and it's not meant to be ... it's just fun.

As with dinner, Dorrien seems to have worked out what's important for a vacation in the snow and what's not – like the big roaring fire in the original eighteenth-century stone fireplace of the bar that awaits the first skiers to return in the late afternoon; or the tea and cakes to go with it; or the fact that the rooms may be old and creaky but the bathrooms are all large, new, clean and – most importantly – have a real bath.

But what about the skiing? From Morzine you have access to the Portes du Soleil, one of several claimants to the title of largest skiable terrain in the world. Once out there, you won't give a moment's thought to the competition.

---

address Le Mas de la Coutettaz, Chemin de la Coutettaz, 74110 Morzine

telephone (33) 4 50 79 08 26 **fax** (33) 4 50 79 18 53

room rates from FF 1,100 (suites from FF 1,600)

le domaine de la baronnie

St-Martin is the kind of town that makes you want to buy a 2CV, learn to play *boules*, and never again drink anything but wine. Beautifully built and beautifully situated, it is the old capital of the Île de Ré, a twenty-mile island off the coast of La Rochelle. With fortifications and an ornate entry designed by Vauban, engineer to Louis XIV, St-Martin is a perfectly preserved fishing port. Unlike other famous ports (such as St-Tropez), tourism has not yet turned every beautiful building here into a Body Shop or a Gap. The old centre remains largely residential. It has a Place de la République, a harbour crammed with fishing boats, lots of elegant eighteenth-century mansions, and original cobblestone streets.

The island traditionally made its living from oysters, salt and wine. Today its charms attract plenty of Parisians, but in the past it was the Dutch and the English who were most interested in its wealth and strategic location. The English were particularly unwelcome. Time and again they tried to capture Ré, but without success. The Duke of Buckingham was most persistent. He laid siege to St-Martin, and came close to triumph: the town's bread supplies ran out on the very day that Louis XIII's reinforcements arrived. The aggressive

intentions of the English were never forgotten. Even today the women who work the salt marshes in the north of the island wear a hat of folded cloth called a *quiche notte*, which derives from the English 'kiss me not'.

The attitude towards foreign visitors is largely academic since for the most part the Île de Ré serves as a weekend retreat for Parisians. But that does not mean it is dominated by hotels and high-rise apartment buildings – quite the opposite. Church steeples and lighthouses are the only structures higher than two storeys. This no-nonsense, unpretentious island enjoys the official status of a protected historic treasure, and restrictions on development are blessedly severe.

If St-Martin is the most beautiful village on Ré, its most beautiful house is without doubt the Domaine de la Baronnie. Proprietors Pierre and Florence Pallardy are not *Retais*, as the locals are known, so they harbour no resentment of the English. Here Italians mingle easily with the ubiquitous Parisians and, yes, even the odd *rosbif*.

This stone house, located around the corner from the thriving port, was built in 1700 on the site of the château of the medieval barons of Ré. Behind its impressive gate is a

tree-lined drive that leads to a court in front and a substantial garden behind. When the Pallardies took it on it was a noble ruin. Since World War II it had been owned by a wealthy bachelor who would spend August each year on Ré with his Portuguese maid. The rest of the time it stood empty. He came less and less as he grew older, and had little reason to keep the house on, but it was never put on the open market. The Pallardy family would not have bought it if it hadn't been for a chain of events that began with an unlikely encounter in the nearby town of Flotte.

Pierre Pallardy is well known in France as the healing osteopath with the magic hands, and his model wife is equally famous. They were drowning their sorrows one afternoon in Flotte after a disastrous property deal when, despite his dark mood, Pallardy couldn't resist asking why the bistrot owner limped. He promptly offered to treat the problem. Some manipulation of the man's ligament produced a miracle. The healed proprietor had overheard

their talk and was eager to repay his debt. Hence they were privy two years later to a whisper that the old man with the Portuguese maid might be prepared to sell, though only to a buyer he trusted to keep the place intact and restore it to the highest standards. Negotiations took a year, but the Pallardies eventually won out.

The Domaine de la Baronnie thus became the house of *bien être*. Here you can benefit not only from the salty air and nearby beaches but from the healing hands of Pierre Pallardy, who has set up a clinic in one of the outbuildings. Guest rooms are suitably baronial: vast suites with high ceilings, decorated with eclectic combinations of fleamarket and auction antiques found by Florence. And for those who cannot keep away from the sea, there's even a widow's-peak duplex suite that features a bedroom in a lookout upstairs where once upon a time the lady of the house would have been found keeping an eye on the Atlantic waiting for her seafaring husband to return.

address Le Domaine de la Baronnie, 21 rue Baron de Chantal, 17410 St-Martin-de-Ré

telephone (33) 5 46 09 21 29 **fax** (33) 5 46 09 95 29

room rates from FF 850 (suites from FF 1,000)

le chat botté

Despite Île de Ré's reputation as one of the most popular summer escape destinations in France, it is not just a holiday isle. There is a year-round population here of around fourteen thousand, spread over some ten communities.

The local *Retais* are descendants of the families who first settled the island and prospered from its traditional sources of wealth, namely salt, oysters and wine. Big trading schooners used to leave Ré loaded with salt and wine, headed for the ports of the Baltic, the New World and anywhere in between. Since a fifth of the island's surface area is marshland, the island's salt productivity is no surprise. The market value of sea salt was once so great that it was called white gold, and it was a source of considerable wealth for the islanders in the Middle Ages and beyond. Today the salt continues to be worked by a few families using the same tools and techniques as their forefathers. Thus unlike many purpose-built island resorts, Ré has a historical heritage that continues to shape its culture independently of contemporary tourism.

One such old *Retais* family are the Massés, who dominate the tourist trade of St-Clément-des-Baleines. This former lobster-fishing village is divided into the five hamlets of

Tricherie, Chabot, Griveau, Gillieux, and Godinand. Set around the old church square, Chabot is the furthest community from the new two-mile toll bridge that connects the island to the mainland at La Rochelle. Apart from being one of the most remote settlements on the island, it is also the smallest and quietest. Lying beneath the imposing sixty-foot tower of the Baleines lighthouse, the hamlet of Chabot is also the most Mediterranean in appearance. Its whitewashed houses, eucalyptus trees in the main square, and colourful bougainvillaea blossoms are more evocative of the sundrenched ambience of the Balearics than the Atlantic coast of France. For nature lovers this is also a superb spot. Within walking distance of Chabot's village square is the Combe à l'Eau national forest – with its own beach – and just beyond the lighthouse is the vast stretch of the Conche des Baleines beach, one of the most unspoiled and least crowded on the island.

The Massé brothers operate Le Chat Botté, the finest restaurant in the area, and just down the road is the family's small, quiet and thoroughly refined village hotel. It was their grandfather who first converted this former priest's cottage into an eight-bedroomed hotel called Chez Florent. Thirty years later his children, Suzanne and Léon Massé, expanded the room count to twenty-three and renamed it Le Chat Botté. In those days it operated solely on a long-stay, full pension basis, with Suzanne working in the kitchens while Léon dealt with the guests. When in 1991 their parents decided it was time to retire, Chantal and Geraldine Massé took up the challenge. They have completely transformed the family hotel in their turn, creating a place of great beauty and charm for those who choose to spend their *vacances* in this quiet corner of the island.

Decorated in soft tones of light grey and beige, the signature style of the hotel is pared-down and pretty. The guest rooms with their *toiles de Jouy* bedspreads, walls of panelled timber and large white bathrooms, look out either onto the church square or the immaculate lawn of the unexpectedly large garden. In style Le Chat Botté is a Gallic version of Laura Ashley gone naive at the beach. It is exactly the kind of place where one could imagine an elegant Parisian woman wishing to while away her summer months. The Massé sisters have given to it an unmistakable air of femininity that is completely in keeping with the charm of the surrounding hamlet.

With this same leisured Parisienne in mind, it's no surprise that the Massé sisters have also introduced a beauty centre at Le Chat Botté. Massages, pedicures, manicures and facials are as much on the agenda as tennis, croquet and some of the best beaches on the island. Oddly enough, the presence of beauticians in their white coats striding purposefully towards their next pampered client only adds to the Frenchness of the whole experience. The beauty centre is open to non-residents too, and judging from the evident popularity of the hotel, the spa and the restaurant, the new generation Massés have continued to make a success of the family salt substitute.

address Le Chat Botté, Place de l'Église, 17590 St-Clément-des-Baleines
telephone (33) 5 46 29 21 93   **fax** (33) 5 46 29 29 97
room rates from FF 370 (*chambres conforts* from FF 630)

le sénéchal

The Île de Ré is like a tiny morsel of the Mediterranean transported to the Atlantic. With a sky like Mykonos and villages resembling those of north Africa, it's not surprising that this island just two and a half hours by train from the Gare de l'Est is so popular with Parisians. Discreet, wild and unspoiled, it's the *sauvage* Yang to Paris's urban Yin. Every summer families abandon their apartments to spend the months of June, July and August amongst the beaches, dunes, marshes and forests of this coastal nature reserve. Île de Ré is all about an anti-urban lifestyle. An extensive network of cycle paths cuts all across the island, small wooden sail boats particular to Île de Ré crowd the harbours and in the old seafaring ports the cafés, brasseries and restaurants are as full as their Parisian counterparts are empty. Mothers and children take up residence in little whitewashed cottages while working husbands commute by TGV at the weekends in anticipation of August, when they too can abandon Paris and go back to nature.

There are many parallels between this isle and the Hamptons on Long Island. Just as East Hampton, South Hampton, West Hampton and Sagaponack serve as a summer escape-valve for New Yorkers, so too does Île de Ré for Parisians. And just like the Hamptons, there are clear distinctions between the different parts of the island and the types they attract. Les Portes, at the furthest tip of Ré, is its most exclusive area (although the large gated houses seem out of step with the island lifestyle); St-Martin the most beautiful; St-Clément the most Mediterranean; and Ars the most artistic.

Nestled in the salt marshes, the village of Ars traditionally prospered from the salt trade. Now the Dutch and Scandinavian vessels that once upon a time crowded the harbour have been replaced by boats made for pleasure not work. Essentially the differences have less to do with appearances than with ambience and attitude. The prevailing attitude of Ars-en-Ré is summed up by the steeple of its medieval church. Visible from miles away, it is painted an unexpectedly stark black and white. The first time I saw it, this struck me as a remarkably modern and graphic thing to do to a church steeple. In fact it was originally painted this way as a signal to the ships of the salt traders making their way to the port of Ars. But practicality aside, it's a splendid piece of modernity and symbolic of the type of people who prefer Ars.

Given the creative bent of the summer residents, Le Sénéchal fits in perfectly. This small hotel is located on one of the town's main streets with a direct view of the modern-gothic spire of the church of St-Étienne. It has artistic attitude stamped all over it. Le Sénéchal is owned, designed and operated by Cristophe Ducharme, an architect from Paris, and his wife Marina. They met and married on Ré and have been regular visitors to Ars for years. The hotel reveals itself by stages – in, for example, the chandelier in the front room by the experimental Dutch design group Droog, or the fabrics by Parisian studio Neotu, their bold and brightly coloured stripes reminiscent of barcodes – or of the striped culottes famously worn by the donkeys of Ré to protect them from the marshland mosquitoes.

All is clean, simple and laid-back, but reveals a touch that could only be that of a very modern-minded architect. This once sad old house has been renovated by the Ducharmes in a design spirit that sits somewhere between minimal and nautical. Rugged floor planks, exposed stone walls and wooden ceilings contrast smartly with the odd flash of luminous colour in the fabrics and cushions and in pieces from the very fashionable and very Parisian gallery Sentou. The stair banisters are made from oars, and guest rooms are furnished with little more complicated than a wicker chair, an industrial lamp and an old cupboard – an artfully simple combination that appeals to the sensibility of the visitors (many of them Parisians who have not yet bought a place of their own on Île de Ré). Not only has the old house been renovated, but more importantly it's been rejuvenated. The staff are young, fresh-faced and friendly, and the place is full of detail that is new and unusual. Le Sénéchal has proven an instant success, particularly with the arty Ars crowd. Actors, writers, photographers and ad-agency people check in for long sojourns because – less predictably for a place of such design vigour – the prices are as bohemian as the crowd.

address Le Sénéchal, 6 rue Gambetta, 17590 Ars-en-Ré

telephone (33) 5 46 29 40 42   **fax** (33) 5 46 29 21 25

room rates from FF 190 (suites from FF 430)

la huchet

Part of La Huchet's attraction is that it is so difficult to find. Getting there can feel like embarking on an old-fashioned treasure hunt. Armed with a rudimentary hand-drawn map, you're faced with at least twenty different ways to get lost. 'Now is that the second path following the bridge immediately after the nudist camp, or the first?' is the sort of thing you are likely to find yourself asking.

The route – if you follow it correctly – takes you through ever smaller towns, as the autoroute from Dax to Bordeaux fades into distant memory. La Huchet really is in the middle of nowhere – but what a nowhere to be in the middle of! Following an extremely narrow and bumpy dirt road through the pine forest – the largest forest in western Europe – you turn a corner to find that the trees have suddenly stopped and you are faced with miles and miles of undulating dunes. You can't see the ocean, you can only hear the faint crashing of the waves beyond the tallest dunes.

Painted red and cream, and constructed in typical Atlantic coast style, La Huchet seems marooned like a shipwreck in the dunes. How did anyone ever come to put a hotel here, you may wonder. The answer is simple: it was only recently converted into a hotel. For two centuries before that it was a hunting cottage (though 'cottage' only in the sense that a Georgian estate is a shack in the English countryside). For the noblemen who came to shoot here, there was clearly a limit to the extent they were prepared to rough it. With twenty-foot ceilings, enormous chandeliers, and fireplaces in every room, it's not exactly your average shooting lodge. And because it was so soundly built, with secure stone foundations, it has survived despite the sandy terrain – which is just as well because the spectacular dunes of Les Landes have long since been a nature reserve and all new building strictly forbidden.

Before Guérard opened La Huchet, the beaches and dunes of Les Landes were largely the preserve of daytrippers and campers. This coastal area on the southernmost Atlantic shores of France lies between Biarritz and the Bassin d'Arcachon. It is defined by endless beaches, towering sand dunes and the white surf of the Atlantic. An hour's drive from Biarritz and a couple from Bordeaux, it's not an area that most French are particularly familiar with, and it's certainly not as popular as Cap Ferret or the Île de Ré further north. A more exclusive destination than La Huchet is hard to imagine.

La Huchet's exclusivity is not just a matter of isolation, however; the hotel also has a unique eligibility programme. Even if you could find it, you couldn't just call, book and drop in. For the only way to stay at La Huchet is to have stayed first at one of Michel Guérard's operations in Eugénie-les-Bains. Guérard set up La Huchet believing that his guests might appreciate a spell on the beach before returning to the real world following the intensive spa treatments at Eugénie-les-Bains. It's an attractive proposition – first you purify and spoil yourself in the green surroundings of Eugénie, with its beautiful gardens, natural hot springs and Guérard's acclaimed cuisine; then, when you're all exfoliated, massaged, mud-bathed and burnished to a glow, you take your Jolly Roger map and lose yourself for a few days among the sand dunes of the Atlantic.

Since La Huchet accommodates a maximum of ten people, it is never a crowded experience. Christine Guérard's design makes the place feel more like a private beach compound than a hotel. In fact you are only reminded that this is a hotel by the welcome bits – the immaculate service, the delicious cuisine and the freshly ironed linen, which, in this case, really is linen. And with Guérard as proprietor, you would be right to imagine that the food goes far beyond the standard of your average beach shack.

The aristocratic proportions of all the guest rooms are suitably grand, while the furnishing style creates the feel of an old, moneyed beach house by its clever mix of sober seaside simplicity, colonial souvenirs from Indochina and lots of rustic ephemera. But most impressive of all are the two beach lofts set in separate, smaller pavilions adjacent to the main lodge. Misleadingly simple from the outside (they look like sun-bleached storage huts), they have twenty-six-foot-high ceilings, open fireplaces, a separate mezzanine for children accessed by a wrought-iron spiral staircase, and the enormous bathrooms that have become a signature of Guérard's approach to hospitality.

---

address La Huchet (Les Maisons Marines d'Huchet), 40560 Vielle Saint-Girons

telephone (33) 5 58 05 05 05   fax (33) 5 58 51 10 10

room rates from FF 3,500 (suites from FF 4,500)

la ferme aux grives

A spa is for wimps, or so I always thought. Why go voluntarily to a place where they wake you up too early, starve you and put you through the kind of drills normally inflicted on new army recruits? Paying for the privilege of being tired, uncomfortable and hungry was what I thought it was all about. That is until I stayed in the spa village of Eugénie-les-Bains.

The French idea of a spa, it turns out, is something quite different. Take, for instance, the food. The proprietor of La Ferme aux Grives (along with the spa facilities and several other operations in Eugénie-les-Bains), is Michel Guérard. Guérard is not just a chef, he's an institution: winemaker and author of countless bestselling cook books, his three Michelin stars go further back than most people can remember. Yet he's not one to rest on his laurels. His continuing success is based on his continuing innovation. He was one of the first big-name chefs in France to embrace the link between being healthy and eating healthily. Like his contemporary, Alain Ducasse, he places the emphasis of his culinary creations on the quality and freshness of the ingredients. His dishes appear simple but are in fact extraordinarily refined. A good example is his signature starter, an 'egg' served just like a

boiled breakfast egg, complete with toast soldiers for dipping – except in this case the 'white' is a mousse of cod fish and the 'yoke' a spoonful of Sevruga caviar. It's a sophisticated combination presented in a surprising manner with subtle variations of taste, texture and ingredients. And for dessert don't miss Guérard's strawberry tart – the most memorable dessert I've ever eaten. Somehow he seems to magnify the taste of today's bland strawberries.

For people who come to a spa to lose weight, you might think that cuisine like this is like having a cigar bar in a smokers' clinic. But Eugénie-les-Bains is a serious spa, with a full-time team of doctors on hand. The key to their dietary approach is balance and proportion. You may feel like you're indulging yourself, but all the while, behind the scenes, there's a great deal of calorie counting and nutritional analysis going on. It's a totally stress-free experience: you, the guest, don't have to give a thought to what you are eating. They do all the worrying for you.

The treatments at Eugénie don't put you to much effort either. Set in a converted farm, the *Ferme Thermale* specializes in cures conceived with the same inventive spirit as the food.

La Ferme aux Grives, where Empress Eugénie once spent the night, is now divided into four sumptuous apartments

The entire complex of Eugénie-les-Bains is built around the gardens, the village's central feature

Even the stoves in Michel Guérard's kitchens were custom-made, with signature neoclassical detailing

The famous spa facilities of Eugénie are housed in an old farm set in a field of immaculately clipped grass

The dining room of Les Prés d'Eugénie, has had three Michelin stars since the late sixties

The enormous custom-made baths with neoclassical splashbacks are typical of Christine Guérard's elegant design

Michel and his wife Christine, for instance, devised their 'white mud' bath based on kaolin (a clay normally used in porcelain) in an exhaustive series of laboratory experiments. The mud is apparently very good for skin problems, and the treatment requires you to do nothing more strenuous than lower yourself into a Roman-style mosaic-tiled sunken bath filled with what looks like melted vanilla ice cream. After this 'ordeal' you are escorted to a barn-like space called the 'recovery room' to recline on one of Christine Guérard's exquisitely designed, colonial-inspired teak *chaises longues*, while the staff 'force' you to drink their (delicious) *tisane* – a mix of herbal teas and fruit juice served cold.

Quite aside from its food and spa, Eugénie also happens to be an idyllic place to escape to. Set in the foothills of the Pyrenees, an hour and a half from the Atlantic coast, it is exactly the kind of picture-postcard village you see all the time in French car commercials but rarely in real life. Miles away from the nearest large town or major highway, this is a countryside of crinkly roads, vineyards, farms and rolling hills.

To cater for different tastes and budgets there is a range of places to stay in the village of Eugénie-les-Bains, but La Ferme aux Grives remains top of my list. The Empress Eugénie, wife of Napoleon III (whose fondness for the healing waters here gave the village its name), is said to have once spent the night in this old farmhouse. Decorated by Christine Guérard in her signature style, it has been divided into four spacious apartments, each with its own living room. The house staff not only service the rooms and prepare breakfast in the downstairs kitchen (called the *chocolaterie*) but are also on hand should someone want afternoon tea in the main salon. All in all it's a thoroughly indulgent set-up – yet another way the Guérards have devised to spoil their guests.

Sadly, it's clear to me now that the toughest thing you will ever have to do at Eugénie-les-Bains is leave.

---

address La Ferme aux Grives, 40320 Eugénie-les-Bains

telephone (33) 5 58 05 05 05   fax (33) 5 58 51 10 10

room rates from FF 2,180 (suites from FF 2,600)

château d'aiguefonde

Is it still possible, despite the popularity of France, to experience its traditional rural charm – to enjoy the beauty, mystery and history of the French countryside without having to share it with busloads of others? The answer is a resounding 'yes!' Provence, admittedly, may be a bit congested since Peter Mayle exposed its charms, but other bits of the French *campagne* are still quite unspoiled and even under-discovered.

The Languedoc fits this bill perfectly. Idyllically situated in the south of France, not much more than an hour's drive from Toulouse and Carcasonne, it is nonetheless little known. Even serious Francophiles can be hard-pressed to tell you where it is. Yet the appeal of the area dates back more than two thousand years. Aiguefonde, in a strategic setting at the foot of the Montagne Noire, was originally an important Roman outpost. The Romans called it Aqua Fonda or 'fountainhead' because it was blessed with an abundance of natural springs and a sweeping view of the entire valley of the River Thorne.

The natural springs are still there today, as is the view, though not much remains of the Roman settlement. In its place is the small village of Aiguefonde, which dates from the thirteenth century. Its castle was built on the Roman foundations. The first *seigneur* of the Château d'Aiguefonde was a powerful noble named Isarn Bonhomme, and his descendants managed to stay in residence there for more than three centuries – quite an achievement given the havoc the religious wars were wreaking upon the French countryside at the time. The high point for the Bonhomme clan undoubtedly came in 1586 when Henri de Navarre, the French Protestant king, was a guest. The elegant and imposing east-wing tower dates from this period.

Aiguefonde changed hands for the first time in 1622 when it was sold to the d'Esperandieu family, who inhabited the château for the next two and a half centuries. In 1770 Jean Louis d'Esperandieu embarked upon a major building programme. His alterations have survived unchanged to this day. They include the formal *Jardin à la Française* designed by André Le Nôtre (better known as the creator of the gardens of Versailles), the entry hall with a double staircase (an *escalier d'honneur*), the long galleries, the French windows, the frescoes (depicting the four seasons), and the very unusual yellow *faux marbre* walls of the library.

From the main entrance hall of Château d'Aiguefonde you can catch a glimpse of the lobby and its original frescoes

A cascading series of waterfalls – the *Rivière à la Russe* – is just one of the property's spectacular water features

In the library, the *faux* marble frescoes uncovered under layers of panelling, contrast with the Vermeer-like floor

After ten years of restoration work, the neoclassical form and symmetry of Le Nôtre's designs have been recreated

A five-course *menu de dégustation* is served nightly under a fine Dutch painting in the intimate dining room

The classical marble statues were installed by Le Nôtre in the eighteenth century

Guest rooms are very Dutch in their crisp decoration and very French in their scale and grandeur

The steep descent (helped by a few buried pumps) accounts for the spectacular height of the water jets

Stark but stylish: an antique Dutch chair upholstered in deep green velvet below another magnificent old master

Adjacent to the château is a formal *Jardin à la Française* designed by André Le Nôtre, no less

Unexpected combinations of furniture and *objets* make Château d'Aiguefonde anything but predictable

The English park is full of hidden spaces, overhanging trees and sun-dappled pathways

he main hall, with its brass chandelier and marble tiles, also serves as a reception lobby

The fountains in the English park were modelled on famous fountains of Peterhof Palace near St Petersburg

The lacquer work hanging above the bath was by proprietor Paul de Vilder, also an accomplished artist

At the far end of one of the garden's rraces is a small green alcove that is a popular spot for afternoon tea

The light-filled library has distinctive yellow and black frescoes and views over the splendid pool and English park

When Paul de Vilder purchased the château, the marble statues were buried by the weeds of decades of neglect

By the time this work was completed in 1819 little remained of the castle's defensive structure – but by then luxurious living had become the new religion; the château was no longer a fort but a grand and sumptuous setting for the good life.

In this respect not much has changed. Chateau d'Aiguefonde has kept not only its gardens, architecture, period details and sweeping view, but it has also preserved the eighteenth-century commitment to fine living. Aiguefonde is all about beauty, both manmade and natural, and the enjoyment of fine food and wine. There is an English park at the rear of the property with its *Rivière à la Russe*, spectacular fountains modelled on those at the Peterhof Palace near St Petersburg. Just beyond are the steep, densely wooded slopes of the Montagne Noire and below is the valley of the River Thorne with its craggy cliff-like banks. Guests are not prompted into activities, and many opt for doing very little, enjoying the long hot summers of this region and biding their time until the host and proprietor, a Dutch artist named Paul de Vilder, darts into the kitchen to exercise his culinary skills. Every night a five-course *menu de dégustation* is served in the small dining room or on the terrace by the swimming pool. The fact that there are only eight rooms means that there will never be more than sixteen guests at dinner. But what really makes Aiguefonde unique is the design signature that Paul de Vilder has brought to the place. There's a distinct touch of Vermeer to the interior. The black-and-white tiles, the plush green velvet on massive oak chairs, and the brass chandeliers, not to mention a superb collection of Dutch old master paintings, bring an element of Holland's Golden Age to the Languedoc.

It's a crazy combination – English parks, Russian fountains, French gardens and Dutch art – but it works. Together with the perfect weather of southern France and the seclusion of the Languedoc, it makes a very seductive alternative to a holiday in Provence.

---

address Château d'Aiguefonde, 81200 Aiguefonde

telephone (33) 5 63 98 13 70 **fax** (33) 5 63 98 69 90

room rates from FF 1,000 (suites from FF 1,250)

hôtel le corbusier

Unité d'Habitation was Le Corbusier's big opportunity to put all his theories on urban housing to the test. Marseilles had been badly bombed during the war. The Vieux Port was all but destroyed and the city authorities were willing to consider all sorts of suggestions for rebuilding, especially for providing urgently needed housing. Thus Le Corbusier finally got his chance to realize his dream of a vertical city. Unité d'Habitation was so named because it was to provide under one gigantic roof all the ingredients for a healthy, happy urban life. If that sounds utopian, it's because the twentieth-century modernists were. Theirs was not architecture for well-endowed foundations or wealthy privileged clients. They were interested in improving the way common people lived.

Le Corbusier's plan was for a building that would house 370 apartments, a kindergarten, a baby crèche, a gymnasium, a supermarket, a restaurant, a bar, a boulangerie … and a hotel. Not only was it built exactly according to these ideas, but, better still, it has stayed that way. The paddling pool on the roof remains a big hit with the kids, the crèche still cares for the building's resident infants, the boulangerie bakes the croissants served in the hotel, elderly gents play *pétanque* in the park, and the hotel

is still operated by the same family that opened it upon the building's completion in 1954.

All too often modernist architecture has become a joke, a chance for the pooh-poohers of the world to point an accusing finger and say 'see, I knew it wouldn't work'. But here's a building that does. There is a quality of calm that suggests people are very content to live here. The odd conversation with residents reveals that this is more than true. The manager of the hotel grew up in this building. His elderly father and mother still live in the duplex apartment they moved into shortly after returning from Indochine. Like many of the apartments, theirs retains its original interior. The compact kitchen with its stainless counter and splashback and blond timber cupboards is not so different from what we might choose today. With a double-storey living room, a lightweight steel staircase, concealed radiators, and large windows with spectacular views, these apartments are also packed with the kind of mod cons that we expect, but that fifty years ago would have seemed incredibly futuristic.

Le Corbusier even predicted the trend for fast food. For a long time the residents could order dinner from the restaurant on the third floor via a specially designed dumb waiter.

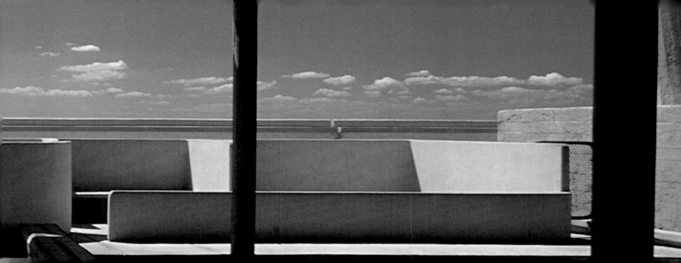

Le Corbusier's comma-shaped parabolic reflective lamps are installed throughout the building

The roof was designed as a playground, complete with paddling pool, fantastic view and this outdoor theatre

In-built fast food: the curved steel box is a dumb waiter connected to the restaurant kitchens

The hotel was part of Le Corbusier's original masterplan for l'Unité d'Habitation

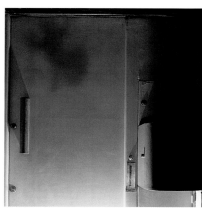

The internal doors are painted in the same bold colours as the exterior: red, green, blue or yellow

In Corb's utopian vision, the ground space saved by the vertical city was to be used for a verdant park

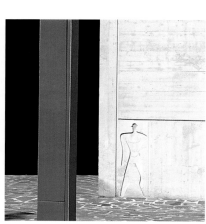

The building was designed according to Corb's 'Modulor', a theory of proportion based on the human form

Unité's history is told in the lobby. During construction it was dubbed 'La Maison du Fada', house of the loony

The standing figure upon which Le Corbusier's 'Modulor' system was based is a recurrent decorative motif

Funnel-shaped towers and organic forms have kept Le Corbusier's design fresh

Corb didn't plan to paint the exterior panels; this was done to disguise the disappointing quality of the concrete

Rhythmic repetitions of shape and colour mean Unité d'Habitation is never boring or overpoweringly immense

Many of the apartments retain their original interiors, and have always been popular with the residents

In the afternoons Le Corbusier worked at his architecture; in the mornings he worked at his art

A mass of green surrounds the building. These tall cypress pines screen the side facing the sea

The entire structure is raised off the ground by massive pillars, creating a feeling of lightness and space

The brightly coloured doors open onto a very wide and very black corridor, which Le Corbusier conceived as a street

The entrance to Unité d'Habitation is covered by a great wing-like expanse of concrete

Sadly, this delivery service is no longer economically viable, but it's one of the few things that have changed. The most important elements have not. The park and the view are among the most powerful attractions of this vertical community. And community is the right word. People are polite, there's no graffiti, no noise, and everyone from single mothers to teenagers and old bachelors seems to love living here.

Architecture magazines and countless books have documented every conceivable statistic about Unité – so many tonnes of concrete, so many cubic metres of granite, so high, so wide, so many tonnes of load – but none has articulated its real success. For that you have to put down the tape measure and camera and stop to talk to the teenager with the skateboard in the lift or the young mothers sunbaking themselves on the roof. The experience of this building is not just for people who are passionate about architecture – it's for people interested in humanity.

Still, do not expect luxe of your accommodation, or even startling modernity. These hotel rooms are fifty years old, and it shows. Le Corbusier would have been the first to admit that the concrete is not perfect: that's why he painted the external panels in different colours, so as to draw attention away from the disappointing quality of their surfaces. Nevertheless, the rooms are spacious and clean, and the bathrooms are white and up to date. The hotel was part of Le Corbusier's original masterplan, and that makes it all the more engaging. Almost all of the facilities of the building are open to the hotel guests. And, as it should be, the hotel is also very affordable. At 225–450 francs per night it makes a good base from which to explore the south of France. Some of the rooms are studios complete with kitchens, and long-term tenancy is certainly not out of the question. An apartment designed by Le Corbusier overlooking the bay of Marseilles for less than 4,000 francs a week – *pas mal*.

---

address Hôtel Le Corbusier, 280 boulevard Michelet – 3ème étage, 13008 Marseilles

telephone (33) 4 91 77 18 15 **fax** (33) 4 91 16 78 28

room rates from FF 225 (studios from FF 325)

michel bras

Welcome to Wyoming. Yes, you are still in France, but this is the Aubrac. The canyons, deserted landscape, and vast horizon here are all uncannily reminiscent of Wyoming.

Michel Bras is of the Aubrac. He was born here, he was raised here, and he works here. More than that, as he says, 'the Aubrac courses through my veins'. Above all the region has profoundly influenced his cooking. Bras is a remarkable chef in a remarkable location. To achieve three Michelin stars in France is no mean feat; to do so in the middle of and in the style of such a remote part of the country is unique.

The Aubrac is the unknown alpine region of France. The Savoie and the Haute Savoie get all the attention and all the tourists; the Aubrac gets to remain unspoiled. This is an area with a thousand miles of white-water rivers and waterfalls, fifteen lakes, mountains for hiking, canyons for climbing, and countless winter ski trails cut into its densely forested slopes. Yet even many French people haven't heard of it, much less been there.

The characteristics of this land are at the very core of the unique culinary experience that Michel Bras offers. His hotel invites you not just to see the beauty but to taste the area.

It sounds a little bizarre, but it works. Almost everything you eat and drink *chez* Michel Bras is deeply characteristic of this region. Some of the dishes are local in origin, such as *aligot*, a deliciously unusual version of mashed potato made with cheese, which is so elastic you have to cut it with a knife. Other dishes are inspired concoctions of local products. Bras' signature dish, *gargouillou de jeunes légumes*, is the perfect example: a colourful still life made from local wild flowers, vegetables and herbs. It is Aubrac on a plate. All the milk used in sauces and desserts is from Aubrac herds and has a famous, slightly aniseed taste produced by the large quantities of wild fennel that the cows consume.

Bras explains that it was his mother who taught him the local secrets of taste and flavour. Oddly enough, Bras' cooking reminds me of Le Corbusier. Corb had strong ideas about everything, including food. He too was a fan of distinctive tastes, and objected most of all to blandness. Michel Bras is the same. He loves anything crisp, crackly, crunchy, sharp or sweet, and adorns his dishes with different textures and flavours. He is part artist and part scientist. Even his research is pursued with laboratory-style thoroughness.

Michel Bras is perched on a hilltop. The sublimely minimal bedrooms are not about furniture but about the view

The brutal simplicity of Michel Bras reflects the harsh and rugged character of this wild, under-discovered area

The decor, like the cuisine, is all local inspiration: the bovine forms of the chairs invoke Aubrac's famed dairy cows

The architecture took its cue from the long, low, rectangular structure of the region's typical farmhouses

Even the table-setting is of the area: Michel Bras is outside Laguiole, famous in France as a centre of knife-making

The no-nonsense local mentality is reflected in the almost Japanese severity of the hotel's minimalist aesthetic

Take for instance his obsession with sugar. How could something, Bras argues, that had long been a nurturing foodstuff, a source of joy in daily food, suddenly be so terribly bad for us? His own research led him to the conclusion that it was not sugar *per se* that was the culprit but modern refinement processes. On the island of Mauritius he discovered a sugar that was still produced in the old-fashioned way. This was found to have seven hundred times the nutritive value of common household sugar. His restaurant now uses this Mauritius sugar exclusively, in its four varieties: white, caramel, dark brown and black.

Clearly Bras is an innovator, and the architecture of his hotel confirms it. It has been likened to a spaceship sitting on a hill, but in fact – like everything Bras is connected with – the building takes its shape, its lines and its raw materials from local sources and traditions. This is tough and uncompromising country, and what at first may seem an indulgence in contemporary design is actually closely related to the spirit of the region. The shape of the bedroom pavilions for instance is based on the *buron*, the basic local farming hut. The granite used in construction surfaces in clumps throughout the countryside: they say in the Aubrac that whenever you see a stone sticking out of the ground there's an entire field of granite below it. Even the path between the buildings housing the guest rooms is an ancient mountain track. Everything at Michel Bras is there for a reason, but nowhere is that reason obvious; like the small mountain wild flowers, to find it you have to look hard. But there's an overall logic and intent that is firmly rooted in the region – you can taste it in the food, and see and feel it in the architecture.

The true appeal of staying chez Michel Bras is perfectly articulated by the grand chef himself: 'People have long overlooked this area, finding it austere. For us, it has simply remained unspoiled. We were born here and we chose to stay here at a time when few were responding to nature's appeal.'

address Michel Bras, Route de l'Aubrac, 12210 Laguiole

telephone (33) 5 65 51 18 20 **fax** (33) 5 65 48 47 02

room rates from FF 1,060 (suites from FF 1,850)

hôtel la pérouse

Nantes was once known as the Venice of the west. Situated at the point where the rivers Erdre and the Loire converge, it was the largest and most important port on the French Atlantic coast. Ships from France's Caribbean colonies and the trading ports in the Far East docked here with their exotic timbers, coffee, tea, Chinese porcelain and spices. Surrounded by water and built on a collection of islands in the Loire, Nantes became one of the most powerful and wealthy cities in France. Its merchants and ship owners built beautiful stone houses along canals and quays that were developed in a similar manner to Amsterdam (though sadly have since largely been filled in). And even before that, Nantes had been a significant medieval centre and the seat of the rulers of independent Brittany, the last of them the famous Duchess Anne. Prosperous and fiercely independent, Brittany has continually threatened secession ever since, and there survives strong separatist sentiment there today.

As in most places with a history of great affluence, culture has long flourished in Nantes. The city invested above all in architecture, establishing a tradition of impressive public as well as private buildings that continues to this day with projects such

as Jean Nouvel's recently completed, ultra-modern Palais de Justice. It's no surprise that such a worldly, wealthy city was the birthplace of Jules Vernes. A place with such strong links with the furthest corners of the earth was the perfect incubator for Vernes' futuristic and global vision.

The history of Nantes is important in understanding a hotel like La Pérouse, for it helps to account for the presence of such an incredibly avant-garde architectural hotel in a provincial city. Nantes is a good place for architects. The citizens it seems are unafraid of progress or vision. Thus it was that M. and Mme Lemonier commissioned local husband and wife architectural duo Clotilde and Bernard Barto – or Barto and Barto as they are known professionally – to design a small hotel right in the centre of the city.

The first thing that strikes you about La Pérouse is that it looks like it's about to fall over. It is a monolithic block of French limestone whose walls are punctuated by horizontal windows looking like an orderly arrangement of giant letterboxes. But these walls are not vertical – they run up and outwards. From the ground, their slightly disconcerting lines greatly amplify the presence

of the building. They were conceived to mimic the leaning angles of the city's old buildings. As Bernard explains, 'For us it was not a choice between historical pastiche or glass tower, but a matter of devising an appropriate urban insertion that echoes historical qualities without copying them verbatim.' The question was not whether La Pérouse would be pretty, he says, but of how one approaches construction at the start of the twenty-first century in the heart of an ancient town.

Perhaps the single most impressive characteristic of La Pérouse is the total lack of compromise. Like it or loathe it, the architects didn't pull any punches. Everything from the steel entrance lamp to the sparsely furnished lobby and even the furniture itself very clearly came directly off the architects' drawing boards. Instead of closets there are glass cubes on casters. Washbasins in the clear-glass mosaic-tiled bathrooms are elongated troughs also fashioned from heavy-duty glass, and instead of curtains or blinds there are

quilts (black on the outside, white on the inside) that button in nautical fashion onto the interior surface.

All this ingenuity is not everyone's cup of tea. It demands the most rigorous visual discipline because nothing else goes with it. Even the odd pot plant or travel brochure would be out of place. La Pérouse is not a hotel for the unadventurous. Aesthetics aside, it has no bar and no restaurant, so the guests have to venture out and find places to eat and drink. In Nantes, however, that is not a problem. Centuries of wealth have created an enviable lifestyle infrastructure. The vineyards surrounding the city produce the famous Muscadet – the third most consumed white wine in the world – and the city has always been a centre of gastronomical excellence. La Cigale, on the Place Graslin, is one of the most opulent brasseries in France, and if a table there is out of the question you can try the smaller and often better restaurants on the rue Jean-Jacques Rousseau in the old quarter.

address Hôtel La Pérouse, 3 allée Duquesne, 44000 Nantes
telephone (33) 2 40 89 75 00 **fax** (33) 2 40 89 76 00
room rates from FF 440 (suites from FF 520)

hôtel de la baume

Half Latin, half Andalusian, Nîmes is possibly the most fascinating town in France. It has all the weather, food and lifestyle of Provence, but a sophistication, beauty and history that is unsurpassed by any other city in the Midi.

Usually I am not much for sightseeing. The notion of standing in line with hundreds of running-shoe-clad, camera-carrying tourists to gawk at a building that has already been totally overexposed in postcards, magazines, books and brochures fills me more with dread than enthusiasm. Nîmes is different. Although Arles was the capital of Roman Gaul, it is in Nîmes that one can really grasp the extraordinary feats of ancient Rome. I would even go as far as to say that the Roman architectural legacy in Nîmes surpasses that of Rome itself. For though Rome may have the Colosseum, for instance, Nîmes has an amphitheatre designed in 100 AD whose thirty-four–tiered construction accommodated 23,000 spectators. This is so well preserved that it is still used for bullfights and other spectacles. Nîmes also has the Maison Carrée built in 5 AD in honour of the sons of the Emperor Augustus. This is one of the best-preserved Roman temples in the world, again largely because it has always been actively in use.

But it is not just its architectural legacy that makes the Roman past come alive. In Nîmes it's the context. It is said that the real key to the success of the Roman Empire was that they understood the role of clean water in civilization. Grasping the link between disease and contaminated water, they exploited their engineering skills to the full to bring clean supplies to their towns. The Pont du Gard just outside Nîmes is perhaps the single most outstanding feat of Roman engineering, and a testament to how far they were prepared to go to supply a town with fresh water. At 900 ft long and 150 ft high (an entire Roman temple could pass through one of its arches), it was part of a thirty-mile long aqueduct bringing water from the source of the Eure near Uzès.

It's possible to connect to the wisdom and achievements of ancient Rome here in a way that feels not a bit touristy. And embracing the Roman roots is a local tradition: citizens of Nîmes have been doing it for centuries. Throughout the old town fragments from the Roman city can be seen incorporated into Nîmes' impressive historic houses, for building stone was continually recycled over the centuries. When in the time of Louis XIV the town embarked on an engineering project to regulate the output of its natural spring, the engineer in charge uncovered the stones of the port of Augustus, one of the original gates in the four-mile walls that surrounded the Roman city. This awareness may have been the catalyst for the town's dedication to architecture in general. For few towns in the world can claim public buildings designed by Jean Nouvel, Norman Foster, Kurokawa, Jean-Michel Wilmotte, and Philippe Starck. From Foster's library and modern art museum opposite the famous Maison Carrée to Starck's design of a bus depot, Nîmes' collection of noteworthy buildings shows a sophisticated, worldly attitude and a conscious intent to blend the ancient and the modern.

This is an attitude typified by Hôtel de la Baume. Situated in the centre of the old town in a narrow street distinguished by more than a handful of noble stone houses, La Baume is a contemporary hotel in the shell of a splendid Renaissance building. Centred around a magnificent labyrinthine seventeenth-century stone staircase, the rooms are timber-beamed, high-ceilinged examples of colourful contemporary design. There is a small breakfast restaurant and bar in the vaulted ground-floor spaces, a courtyard at the base of the staircase, and a beautifully detailed stone entrance from the street. Hôtel de la Baume is not pristine – in fact some might call it a bit shabby – but it is undoubtedly architecturally impressive. In any case Nîmes itself is the real attraction. Apart from its enthralling Roman heritage, the old town is dotted with chic cafés, well-dressed people and handsome shops. And like Arles, the town has bullfighting in its blood. It is said that children here dream of becoming bullfighters rather than footballers or popstars. Some of the world's greatest contemporary artists have been commissioned to produce posters for Nîmes' Pentecost *feria*, including Francis Bacon and Julian Schnabel. Art, architecture, lifestyle, history, culture: Nîmes has it all, squeezed into an area so compact that you will never need to get on a bus.

---

address Hôtel de la Baume, 21 rue Nationale, 30000 Nîmes
telephone (33) 4 66 76 28 42 **fax** (33) 4 66 76 28 45
room rates from FF 480

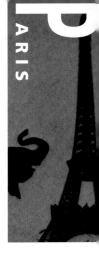

bel ami

'A movable feast' is how Hemingway described Paris. It's an evocative analogy that's still valid today. Many, if not most 'world cities' are now dominated by densely constructed business zones dedicated to work work work, with just the odd institution for enjoyment – whether it be eating, drinking or socializing – scattered throughout as if to provide an escape valve for the pressures of the daily grind. But Paris is the exact opposite.

This city is a concentration of unequalled beauty, character and style devoted to the enjoyment of life, with the odd area dedicated to that grim necessity, work. La Défense, a collection of ultra-modern buildings on the outskirts of the city, is the typically Parisian answer to the requirements of the modern city. It is fundamentally a work zone, but one that is away from centre of the city, keeping historic areas like the Left Bank mercifully free from office blocks. The entire district around the famous Boulevard St-Germain is devoted more to the pursuit of living than the pursuit of money. And despite its enormous popularity with tourists, the Left Bank has lost none of its appeal. How can you tire of the fashion shops on the Boulevard St-Germain or such institutions as the Brasserie Lipp, Café des Deux Magots or Café de Flore? They might be slightly more expensive than some of the city's lesser known cafés and brasseries, but what is remarkable is that against all odds they have managed to preserve not only their identity but also their local clientele. Go for a late lunch on a weekend afternoon in winter at the Café de Flore, for example, and you'll find that the crowd upstairs are mainly Parisian.

What a relief, you say. Paris hasn't been ruined by tourism. The Left Bank is still the place to be. But that's not exactly earth-shattering news. So what is the point? The point is that for the real enjoyment of Paris, location plays a key role, and no hotel is better situated in this respect than the newly opened Bel Ami. You could walk out of Bel Ami's lobby at 8.55 am and be at a table enjoying a legendary *chocolat chaud* at the Café de Flore by nine. This is St-Germain-des-Prés, the absolute heart of Hemingway's Paris, lined with galleries, antique shops, book dealers, and fashion boutiques. Once the haunt of Jean-Paul Sartre, Simone de Beauvoir and all their existentialist cronies, the area still attracts the artists and the intellectuals – even though Emporio Armani and Christian Dior have moved in. The choice of things to see, buy,

eat or drink is quite mind-boggling. And there's always the timeless, effortless alternative of simply sitting outside one of the legendary cafés and watching life go by.

As the third hotel in Paris to get the G.L.A. treatment (that's Grace Leo-Andrieu's hotel management company to the uninitiated), the Bel Ami provides a much-needed alternative to the consistently popular and frequently booked-out Montalembert. Situated in a building that in the eighteenth century housed the national print works churning out parliamentary documents, this former industrial space is now a thoroughly slick exercise in refined and contemporary neutrality. Great expanses of light-coloured marble on the floor, cotton slipcovers and upholstery in shades of light caramel, anis green and dark chocolate, furniture in polished Wenge wood, black-and-white photography, bamboo trees and the odd splash of acid colour: it's all a far cry from the fourteenth century, when Pope Alexander III was able to enter the St-Germain monastery through a doorway situated in the middle of what is now the lobby.

The Bel Ami is the embodiment of the new cutting-edge Parisian style with a dash of Asian minimalism, a signature that has now filtered down to become the most popular choice for the private interiors of the avant-garde community. But as well as being the style of choice for the area's hipper residents, the Bel Ami's chic, pared-down approach is entirely in keeping with the reputation of nearby fashion boutiques, art galleries and design showrooms.

In its interior design the Bel Ami captures absolutely the new Paris – stylish, elegant and sophisticated as ever, but now also understated and utterly smooth. The idea was never to be startlingly different, just young, simple and hip. With 115 guest rooms the hope is that the hotel won't be quite as difficult to book in to as the Montalembert – although considering the enduring popularity of this part of Paris it won't be surprising if it is.

---

address Bel Ami, 7–11 rue Saint Benoît, 75006 Paris

telephone (33) 1 42 61 53 53   **fax** (33) 1 49 27 09 33

room rates from FF 1,550 (suites from FF 3,200)

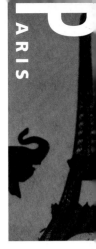

hôtel costes

When the Costes first opened it was quite a phenomenon. It was *the* place to be seen for breakfast, lunch, and dinner. All *le beau monde* of Paris – from the worlds of film, fashion, television, music and publishing – made the Costes their hangout. Even other hotels recommended it as a place to eat out – if you could get a table, that is.

Two years on, the hotel is still the place to meet. If anything the Costes has become an institution. All the sceptics who predicted that the Costes hype was nothing more than a passing trend have been proved wrong. The hotel has successfully made the transition from bright new thing to the more relaxed status of assured favourite.

All of which is good news, particularly for the guests. The atmosphere used to be frantic verging on manic – great for going out, not so great should you want an early night. A quiet evening in was only possible after all the party people had gone home, and every night at the Costes was a party.

Now that the novelty has worn off, the pace is less hectic – it's still very very busy, but it is no longer boiling over. Its continuing popularity as a venue for lunch, dinner or a drink now has more to do with the food and

ambience than the simple fact that it's the newest place in town. This success is vindication for designer Jacques Garcia and his visionary client Jean Louis Costes. Until Garcia came along, the style of the late nineteenth-century Belle Époque was generally disdained by serious critics of the French decorative arts. It was considered too busy, too confused: too much colour, too many patterns and too many disparate influences – Chinoiserie, Rococo, neo-Gothic, *japonisme*, Empire and orientalism among them. But that is exactly why Garcia used it as his design theme. For Jacques Garcia's style preferences are the exact opposite of the modern trend towards simplicity. For him too much is *never* enough. His idiosyncratic and unconventional approach certainly gave the Costes a look and feel that is different from anything else in Paris.

Different is also a key word in the restaurant and hotel empire Jean Louis Costes and his brother have built from the ground up in Paris. Starting with the famous Café Costes in the mid-1980s, which launched the career of superstar designer Philippe Starck, Costes has built his business on the most fundamental truth guiding today's hospitality industry:

people don't want everything to be the same. What would be the fun of travel if it was? The environment Garcia created for Costes is so fascinating because it had to be created absolutely from scratch. It's hard to imagine today, standing in the Agatha Christie–Orient Express-style lobby looking out on a splendid Italianate courtyard, that once upon a time this building had about as much style as your average Novotel.

Garcia is a great enthusiast of French decorative history and he used his knowledge to shape every last detail of the Costes interior. The chairs, the lamps, the carpets, the fabrics, even the classical statues that adorn the courtyard were specially designed and made for the hotel. In an age when we are increasingly accustomed to urban colour schemes of white and more white with just the odd splash of pale colour, Garcia saturated the interior with strong, rich, luxurious shades. Bathrooms are painted deep earthy reds or strong ochre yellows, floors are tiled in Moorish patterns,

chairs are upholstered in rich red silks patterned in stripes, paisleys, and brocades, bedroom walls are papered in bold Victorian florals and paisleys, dining rooms are panelled in gilded wooden *boiserie*, bar stools – oriental in form – are covered in studded acid-green velour. On it goes. Layer upon layer upon layer of colour, pattern, texture and shape create the kind of visually dense environment that you would usually only encounter in a truly historic interior. 'Why do things simply,' jokes Garcia, 'when you can make them more complicated?'

This is certainly not a decor many people would wish to live with, but then that's not the point. For a few nights the Costes is an adventure, a visual vacation from what you're used to. When the lights are turned down and the rich *fin de siècle* setting truly comes into its own, it's a magic place, and even more so because the Parisians themselves love it. That makes being seen at the Costes one of the faster ways to establish your credentials in Paris.

address Hôtel Costes, 239 rue Saint-Honoré, 75001 Paris

telephone (33) 1 42 44 50 00   **fax** (33) 1 42 44 50 01

room rates from FF 2,000 (suites from FF 3,500)

hôtel lancaster

It may have come as a surprise to readers of *Wallpaper* that the magazine recently chose the Lancaster's Marlene Dietrich suite as one of the best hotel suites in the world. With no sixties plastic furniture or icons of modern design, it's not a typical choice for the magazine that has made its name by advocating state-of-the-art architecture and design. Yet it came in at number three in *Wallpaper*'s annual top one hundred. Was this perhaps the beginning of a new editorial direction for the bible of the ultra-cool consumer? *Au contraire*. The accompanying article only reinforced the magazine's commitment to design. As it pointed out, many VIP suites in so-called 'design' hotels leave one with the feeling of having paid an awful lot for very little: no furniture, no antiques, no history, no value for money. In other words, they are the opposite in every way to what was Marlene Dietrich's favourite hotel suite. Decorated entirely in her favourite pinks and mauves, it has a living room with a marble fireplace, Aubusson rugs, a very rare Louis XIV cartel clock, a Louis XV desk placed before a large bay of soaring French windows that overlook a private courtyard garden, and enough space to host a cocktail party for fifty. The adjoining bedroom is exactly right for

Paris. Intimate, feminine and cosy, it overlooks the same courtyard and admits absolutely no trace of the noise and hubbub that is usually inescapable in large metropolitan cities. Elegant, beautiful and timeless, this is all you could want from a hotel suite in Paris.

The Lancaster is the new Ritz. It's where everyone who is anyone wants to stay. But while the Ritz came to fame in the late 1800s by imitating the ostentatious lifestyle of rich society, the Lancaster has made its mark not with grandeur but with discretion. How discreet is the Lancaster? It must be the only five-star hotel in Paris with no public spaces … whatsoever. It has no famous bars, no high-profile restaurants, and no facilities that allow access to non-residents. The only non-guests are either friends of the guests or journalists arriving for pre-arranged interviews with the likes of Quentin Tarantino, Jeremy Irons or Matt Damon, all of whom choose to stay here when in Paris. And unlike so many hotels where the lobby and public areas are by far the most glamorous spaces, the most attractive rooms in this hotel are the guest rooms. Each and every one is different, but what they all have in common – aside from their antique furniture and beautifully proportioned spaces –

IZI

PHOTOGRAPHIES 1944

Photographie
Éditions
de La Martinière

COLLECTION DIMENSIONS

F

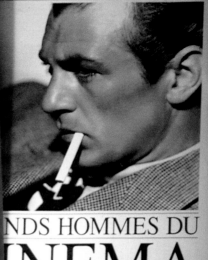

NDS HOMMES DU
NEMA

GRUND

Bridge

JOHN FLATT

CARO
CARL

DELA

KENNETH WHITE

Édité avec la
Centre d'Art, Contem
Centre d'Action
Musée Géo C...
Hexagone Meylan

FLORETTE LARTIGUE

JACQUES-HENRI
LARTIGU
LA TRAVERSÉE DU

are their quirky, unexpected features: a hidden closet, a bathroom with a balcony, or a roof terrace with a view of the Eiffel Tower. Nothing is overdone, nothing too grand. The place oozes aristocratic ease. The Lancaster has become about the most difficult hotel in Paris to get in to – but that of course only adds to the appeal.

The style of the hotel owes much to the collecting zeal of its first owner, Émile Wolf, who went to great lengths to fill his Haussmann-era apartment building with splendid antiques. Countless visits to the Paris auctions and antique markets produced a hoard of Louis XV and XVI chairs, Chinoiserie tables, commodes with neoclassical marquetry, and a collection of antique clocks of a quality and diversity that would be near on impossible to assemble today.

In the early days the hotel was also lucky to count Russian émigré artist Boris Pastoukhoff as a long-term guest. Pastoukhoff never had the money to pay his bill, and thus M. Wolf ended up with about eighty of his paintings. Today the artist's work hangs in some of the world's greatest museums of modern art, but the best single collection of it is displayed through the guest rooms of the Hôtel Lancaster.

Yet in time the hotel suffered the fate of so many grand hotels – it became stuffy, and then it became corporate stuffy under an international chain. Its resurrection came about by the energetic intervention of Grace Leo-Andrieu. Familiar with the Lancaster since her days as vice-president of the Paris Warwick just down the street, she had long dreamed of taking it over. She and her husband Stéphane finally bought the Lancaster in 1996 and embarked upon the modernization it so badly needed. That included restoring the antiques, adding minimal marble bathrooms, and introducing a sense of modernity to complement M. Wolf's superb collection. Today the Lancaster is the very embodiment of the classic Parisian interior that we all dream of experiencing at least once. And with discretion being the new luxury, you can be confident that no-one will ever know that you did.

---

address Hôtel Lancaster, 7 rue de Berri, 75008 Paris
telephone (33) 1 40 76 40 76 **fax** (33) 1 40 76 40 00
room rates from FF 1,167 (suites from FF 4,657)

hôtel montalembert

With their renovation of the Montalembert, completed in 1989, Grace Leo-Andrieu and her husband Stéphane invented a new kind of hotel. Whereas L'Hôtel was one of the original so-called boutique hotels, the Montalembert was a next generation development: the contemporary luxury hotel.

This was something completely different, a five-star hotel with all the trimmings – the goose-down pillows, the chic designer soaps, the super bathroom, the desirable address … all the bells and whistles except one – not a trace of old-fashioned stuffiness. Here was a hotel that was not trying to look like an English club, a French château or an Italian palazzo. It didn't have a theme, unless you could call being simple, smart and elegant a theme.

More than a decade after the debut of this tone-setting hotel, it's still as popular as when it first opened. Why? Because the Montalembert is the Kelly bag of Parisian hotels – beautifully made, practically functional, well designed, and timelessly elegant.

The Montalembert was the launch-pad for a new approach to design in Paris. Through most of the eighties the city was experimenting with fads that had great press but little staying power. First there was the anarchic Memphis introduced by the Italians; then there was the neo-Barbarian twist to Baroque that brought the names Garouste and Bonnetti to the fore. But while it was all very inventive, it had nowhere to go. How long could anyone seriously remain amused by bronze versions of Fred Flintstone's furniture?

With the Montalembert French design began to rediscover its roots. Commissioned by Grace Leo-Andrieu, designer Christian Liaigre introduced an approach that had more to do with French history than with French fashion. As in the times of Louis XIV, XV and XVI, Liaigre returned to fine materials and considered proportions to create furniture of real beauty. Working with exotic woods he revived respect for fine craftsmanship and attention to detail, but – unlike the extravagant French monarchs – he avoided fancy decoration. With the Montalembert French design achieved a new beauty, and the entire hotel industry was shown a new direction.

The goal of the renovation was simple: to integrate a contemporary style with the elegant original architecture. The hotel's collection of antiques was repaired and restored and Liaigre's furniture designs were installed throughout the fifty-one rooms and five suites.

The Montalembert's ground-floor dining space is popular with the art- and antique-dealing crowd of the Left Bank

Banisters, lamps, hat racks and even ash trays were commissioned in bronze and wrought iron from artist Eric Schmitt

The Montalembert's period birdcage li is splendidly Parisian, although a rare sight in the city these days

The ground-floor lobby has the feel of an art gallery: bright, spacious, and punctuated by tribal sculptures

This intimate library with fireplace and comfortable leather armchairs is a popular spot in the winter

Clean and classic: dark timber furniture and bedheads, white walls and navy-striped bedlinen define the guest rooms

Sculptor Eric Schmitt was commissioned to produce the bronze wall lights, stair rail and other details that adorn the hotel throughout.

The result has been an across-the-board success. Design and restaurant guru Terence Conran has declared it his favourite hotel in Paris, and the list of celebrity guests that agree would run to the bottom of this page. Even more significant than the initial success, however, is the way in which the Montalembert has maintained its opening momentum without changing a thing. Leo-Andrieu and Liaigre together seem to have stumbled upon a formula that brings together timeless elegance and contemporary lifestyles. By comparison with other hotels, the public space allocated for such amenities as bar, restaurant and lobby at the Montalembert is tiny. These three blend together without walls or doors in the hotel's limited ground-floor entrance area. The casual and free-flow nature of such an arrangement works very well – better in fact than a series of strictly separate spaces ever would these days. In the morning this tiny public space is set up for breakfast; during the day it is popular with guests and locals who drop in for a light lunch; while in the evening it serves as a meeting place for drinks and afterwards as a chic dinner venue. It feels easy and intimate, like the hotel equivalent of eating in the kitchen. This unenclosed space is both elegant and informal; it is perfect for mobile phones, casual clothes and the modern lifestyle.

The only criticism one ever hears of the Montalembert is that the rooms are on the smallish side. This is true enough, but it must be set against the fact that the hotel enjoys one of the best locations in Paris. Around the corner from the Boulevard St-Germain, in the very heart of the famous antique shops, jewelry boutiques and art galleries of the Left Bank, and just a stroll away from the famous Café des Deux Magots and Café Flore, there is little conceivable reason why anyone would want spend much time in their room.

address Hôtel Montalembert, 3 rue de Montalembert, 75007 Paris

telephone (33) 1 45 49 68 68   fax (33) 1 45 49 69 49

room rates from FF 1,800 (suites from FF 2,950)

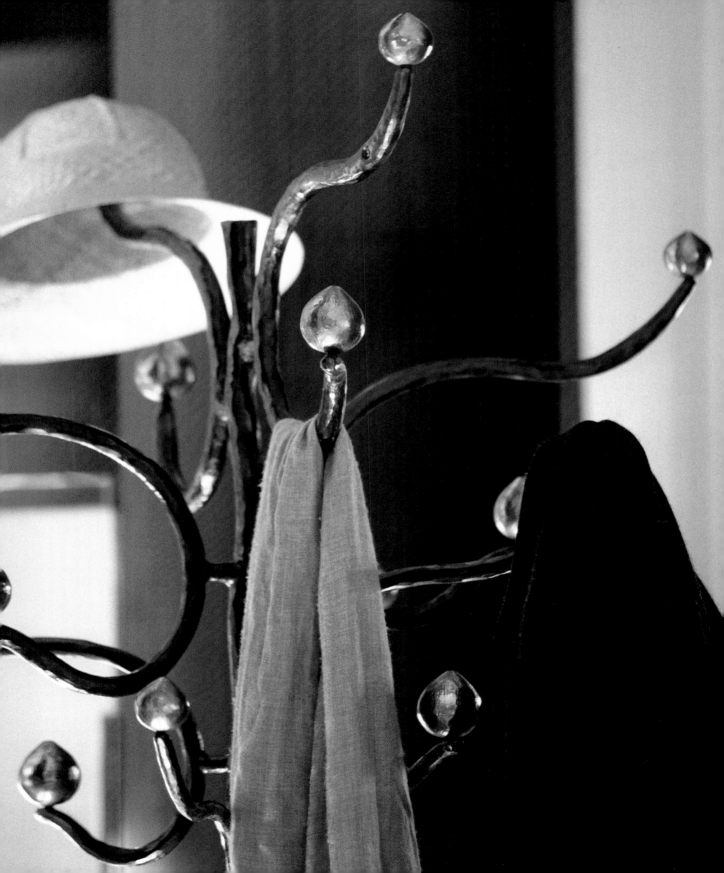

hôtel trocadéro dokhan's

Not everyone who visits Paris is on vacation. As in any big city, many travellers are here for work, and their priorities are rather different. The Left Bank is not that convenient if you have an appointment in La Défense. The struggle of having to cross town first thing in the morning, and then the battle with rush-hour traffic in the afternoon will very quickly sour its charms.

For people who need (or want) to be on the Right Bank, Dokhan's is a very attractive alternative. Situated in the exclusive sixteenth arrondissement, this handsome nineteenth-century limestone building is in one of the most chic areas of Paris. Close to the famous Art Deco Trocadéro, with its fantastic view over the Eiffel Tower, it is also in walking distance of the Arc de Triomphe, the Champs-Élysées, the prestigious Avenue Foch and the sophisticated shopping of Avenue Montaigne. Some of the most beautiful and stately residences in Paris are in this area, and consequently the neighbourhood is full of elegant little restaurants and discreet boutiques.

It's an atmosphere and lifestyle into which Dokhan's blends perfectly. The designer responsible was Frederic Mechiche. Like his colleague Jacques Garcia, Mechiche made his name creating private interiors for high-profile, big-name Parisians, so he's not strictly speaking a commercial designer – but that is what made him such an inspired choice for this hotel. Someone accustomed to designing houses for a sophisticated elite will bring different criteria to the job. What Mechiche gave Dokhan's above all is a seductive mood – precisely the kind of mood people expect from Paris.

Take the hotel's champagne bar, for example. It is entirely panelled in exquisite eighteenth-century *boiserie* – wood panelling that was rescued by Mechiche, re-tailored to fit the space, and painted a most unusual shade of chartreuse green with fine gilded detailing. The result is a space of remarkable character and quality, despite being relatively small. The champagne comes each week from a different vineyard, and the food menu is designed to complement it, with simple dishes like cold salmon and potato. The Dokhan's bar is small, chic and unique: there's nothing else quite like it in Paris. No wonder then that it has become a popular venue with locals for after-hours drinks. And in the morning the space converts to a breakfast room, which especially in winter has an ambience that more than compensates for the grey outside.

Designer Frederic Mechiche is known for his penchant for one-off pieces found in Paris antique markets

Set in a typical Parisian garret, the Bagatelle Suite is all black-and-white patterns with the odd piece of mahogany

Clean but classic: black-and-white mattress ticking, nickel-plated taps and elegant wall lamps in a typical bathroom

The unusual architecture means that each room at Dokhan's is different in form as well as colour and decor

The lobby saloon mixes neoclassical detailing with the odd unexpectedly modern touch, like this Picasso sketch

The Ming Suite, in an attic-style space on the top floor, is a small apartment decorated entirely in Ming blue

What is so convincing in the design of Dokhan's is the overall impression of authenticity. Mechiche's signature fits so comfortably with the architecture that it's hard to believe that everything was stripped to bare bones and created from scratch. The Adam-inspired neoclassical salon, the elegantly panelled reception, the old oak parquet floor, the massive doors, velvet curtains, and black-and-white tiled lobby: the entire ensemble was conceived in Mechiche's imagination.

The most extraordinary guest spaces are on the top floor of this handsome wedge-shaped building. There are four suites that make great use of the gabled and angled attics that are so typical of Paris. Each has its own unique personality. The Ming Suite, for example, is decorated entirely in the blue shades of Chinese porcelain. The focal point of this mini-apartment is the round bed set into the space defined by a single oval window right at the top of the building. Another suite, the Eiffel, is a duplex in tones of beige, gold and black, with a small living room that has an unimpeded view of the Eiffel Tower. And this surprise and intimacy is not reserved to the suites. Because of the building's odd shape, it was possible to create an array of unusual spaces, each with the style and ambience unique to the designer.

Perhaps the biggest surprise of all is that this hotel is part of the Sofitel group. When I first saw the sign, discreet as it is, I was disbelieving. Sofitel, part of the giant hotel group Accor, is not exactly renowned for small, highly individual hotels. But times have changed and in a bid to get more involved in the world of unique hotels they have entered the management contract arena. The deal is simple: the hotel owner creates the character and individuality; Sofitel provide the day-to-day expertise. It's an arrangement that appears to work well. The hotel was created by enthusiasts with vision and is managed by professionals with training and experience. The benefactor is the guest, particularly the guest who also has some work to do while in Paris.

address Hôtel Trocadéro Dokhan's, Sofitel Demeure Hotels, 177 rue Lauriston, 75016 Paris

telephone (33) 1 53 65 66 99 **fax** (33) 1 53 65 66 88

room rates from FF 2,300 (suites from FF 4,500)

l'hôtel

If ever a more detailed attempt is made to investigate the origins of what has now become a worldwide phenomenon – the trend towards highly individual hotels – then this place will certainly feature as a pioneer. It's difficult to convey just how far ahead of its time L'Hôtel was in the sixties. In a period in which chains such as Hilton were successfully luring guests with their blatant uniformity (same room, anywhere in the world), L'Hôtel was investing in total individuality.

The notion of working with a designer to create a unique interior now seems a perfectly sound business strategy, but in those days it was positively risqué. And in fact I doubt whether even today a designer would be given the creative latitude extended to American designer Robin Westbrook. The magnificent round neoclassical stairwell that rises from a star-patterned terrazzo floor would alone have required extensive architectural remodelling to the existing building – never mind the fact that it takes up considerable space, which even then was at a premium on the expensive Left Bank. But design-wise it was just the beginning. The guest rooms took the creative process to an even further extreme. Westbrook was permitted to all but abandon any constraint of convention.

It is as if the classically trained designer discovered LSD, *A Clockwork Orange* and *Sgt Pepper's Lonely Hearts Club Band* all at the same time. Some of the guest rooms are the architectural equivalent of a psychedelic Rolls Royce. One of them has wall-to-wall *faux* leopard skin and matching bedspreads, while another – the Marilyn Monroe room – is all white with mirrored everything, including the bed, the chairs and the vanity desk, plus a red carpet and some very sexy blue silk moire fabric. A tiny, all-red room on the first floor is furnished with predominantly black and gold Empire pieces, with an emerald green marble-clad bathroom. One floor higher, a room clad wall to wall in dark green velvet is contrasted by a bathroom of creamy coloured marble and white bath linen. Yet another Empire room combines an Egyptian-inspired bed with purple carpet and fuchsia walls and the odd touch of gilded detailing. The first time I stayed I was so inspired to experience all these different rooms that I asked the management to move me every night.

Even before its sixties makeover L'Hôtel had a distinguished pedigree. The plaque on the wall outside is dedicated to one no less than Oscar Wilde, who died here in 1900.

The penthouse apartment of L'Hôtel in Paris is a shameless fashion mistake

In the Marilyn Monroe suite, the bed, the tables, the stool, and even the clock are made of mirrors

Mixed in with all the sixties funk is the odd splendid antique – like this baroque mirror decorating one of the landings

e red, white and blue Marilyn Monroe
suite is all white silk, blue satin, red
carpet and an infinity of mirrors

In room 34 *everything* except for the
floor is covered in *faux* leopard skin.
Did anyone say rock star?

Decorate to be noticed:
nothing whatsoever about L'Hôtel
is subtle or understated

Broke, sick, his reputation in tatters, the great wit was still able to summon some inspiration on his death bed when he wrote to a friend: 'I am dying beyond my means'. In his memory L'Hôtel maintains an Oscar Wilde Suite containing mementoes and a few of his final letters – although decoratively its rather cluttered, vaguely Victorian interior and big sleigh bed pale in comparison to some of the others on offer.

Admittedly, some of the rooms have dated rather better than others, but even that has its charm. L'Hôtel is one of the few hotels anywhere in the world that have kept their sixties interiors intact, and with a strong sixties revival currently being championed by style magazines like *Wallpaper*, that is a major attraction. Then there is its location on the rue des Beaux-Arts, surrounded by trendy art galleries and antique dealers in the absolute heart of the fashionable Left Bank. Here it is still possible to imagine yourself in the Beatnik Paris of the sixties. Bring your Carlos Santana CD, hire the red and blue velvet poppy-clad penthouse and enjoy a weekend in a groovy 'sixties' Paris that even the magazines don't know about.

Without a doubt the hotel has seen better days. The vast catacombs under the building were once the location for a funky bar, but these days they are roped off and deserted. Similarly, the space used for breakfast is a bit tired and not in the same league as the rooms. All in all the hotel is a bit of an old swinger in need of another makeover. But the very fact that it has rough edges is part of its appeal. It's a *folie* like nothing else in Paris, and yet somehow utterly at home here. This after all is the very centre of the Paris that Hemingway, Picasso, Man Ray and other icons of twentieth-century culture made their home. For all those archetypally Parisian activities of window-shopping, sitting in cafés and watching life go by, this is still the best place for squeezing the most out of what this uniquely stylish city has to offer.

address L'Hôtel, 13 rue des Beaux-Arts, 75006 Paris

telephone (33) 1 44 41 99 00   **fax** (33) 1 43 25 64 81

room rates from FF 1,800 (suites from FF 3,800)

auberge des glycines

The south of France isn't what it used to be. The property developers have hit paradise hard. Great swathes of the Midi are now very suburban. American-style shopping malls, McDonald's, Pizza Hut and used-car lots have long since cropped up all over towns that were once unadulterated romantic fantasies. But show me a place that is immune to change – or so a realist might retort.

Well, Porquerolles is that place. Located about seven miles off the coast from the port of Hyères, this island, one of the three that form the Îles d'Or (the Golden Isles), has preserved everything that was once taken for granted in the south of France. The reason is simple: since 1971 most of the island has been classified by the French government as a national park. Hence its craggy cliffs, azure blue bays, sandy white beaches, inland forests and handful of vineyards are all mercifully intact. This is the island's most powerful asset. As locals will boast, 'our biggest luxury is nature.' People don't come here to be seen, they come here to hide. Nor are there any cars allowed on Porquerolles, other than the few essential for maintaining services and supplies. In a surprisingly Californian gesture, there's also a very strict non-smoking policy on the

entire island, with the exception of the bars, cafés and restaurants in the village. This is enforced by the deterrent of a very hefty fine.

Still, you might wonder how a small island only twenty minutes off the Côte d'Azur could have escaped the clutches of the developers *before* being classified as a park. The answer lies in its unlikely history. Although it once had some strategic military importance – which explains the presence of a few ruined forts – historically speaking Porquerolles was a bit of a flop. It had a brief stint as a penal colony (a Midi Antipodes?), a gig as an orphanage for juvenile delinquents, and was the short-lived site of an ecologically unfriendly soda factory. Then the entire island was purchased by Belgian entrepreneur François Joseph Fournier as a wedding present for his new bride Sylvia. Fournier had made his fortune in the silver mines of Mexico, and with his resources he proceeded to create Porquerolles in the mould of the giant self-contained haciendas that he had known in Mexico. He completed his own private Eden with fruit groves, vineyards, livestock and hunting game.

Even though the island is now in the public domain, the same Fournier family still plays a big role in Porquerolle's day-to-day affairs.

Lelia Le Ber, François Joseph's daughter, is the mayor; Yves Le Ber, her son, operates La Plage d'Argent, the island's only beach restaurant; and Sebastien Le Ber, his brother, is commodore of the yacht club and patron of his grandfather's wine label, Le Domaine de l'Île.

I can only imagine what the south of France was like in the nineteen-twenties and thirties, but I'd say it wasn't too different from the way Porquerolles is today. The old town is dominated by a simple ochre-coloured church and the dusty unpaved village square is still used for daily games of *pétanque*. At around 6 pm the entire island stops for a *pastis* in any one of its small and charming cafés, and by nightfall the cicadas are the only ones making a racket. Life is simple here – swimming, hiking and exploring during the day, drinking, dining and promenading at night. There are no nightclubs, no boutiques, expensive or otherwise, and best of all no traffic.

Auberge des Glycines fits this scenario perfectly. Simply put, the hotel is exactly like the island: beautiful, colourful, charming, unpretentious and natural. Situated just off the dusty village square, from the outside it is a typical terracotta-tiled, blue-shuttered, bougainvillaea-flanked house of the Midi. At the back is an idyllic vine-clad courtyard that also serves as the summer dining room. Inside the style is old-money summer cottage: lots of straw hats, blue gingham bedspreads, white cotton throws and the odd piece of mismatched furniture – antique cupboards, wardrobes or dressers. The colours too are typically Provençal: terracotta and biscuit on the staircase, whitewashed rooms and an ochre exterior with blue shutters. The restaurant also happens to be one of the best places to eat on the island, serving the aubergines, tomatoes, courgettes, caramelized onions, button mushrooms, and of course the swordfish and sardines that so distinguish the cuisine of the Midi. Auberge des Glycines and the island of Porquerolles really do offer the chance to escape to the south of France as it used to be.

address Auberge des Glycines, 22 place d'Armes, Île de Porquerolles, 83400 Hyères

telephone (33) 4 94 58 30 36 **fax** (33) 4 94 58 35 22

room rates from FF 390

abbaye de la celle

In 1998 Alain Ducasse became the first French chef to operate two three-Michelin star restaurants. Then in 1999 he opened a second hotel in his stomping ground of the south of France. Like the famous Bastide de Moustiers, the Hostellerie de l'Abbaye de la Celle offers a chance to experience the countryside of the Midi. Ever since the Société des Bains de Mer of Monte Carlo invited him to take the position of executive chef at the terribly grand Louis XV in the late eighties, M. Ducasse has been unstoppable. In 1990 he was granted three stars for the Louis XV and in 1997 he achieved the same with the eponymous Alain Ducasse in Paris. Next came Spoon, the restaurant that set all of Paris talking by daring to mix cuisine from all over the world. Other Spoons inevitably followed, one in the Saint-Géran Hotel on Mauritius, and another in Ian Schrager's London hotel Sanderson's.

Recently he also opened Bar & Boeuf in Monte Carlo which was promptly awarded a Michelin star. It's no surprise then that *American Town and Country* magazine called him 'the Titan of Taste'. He has built a gastronomic empire of note in a relatively short period of time. Some American magazines have even gone so far as to describe him as the most influential chef in the world today.

Ducasse was born and raised in Les Landes, the area between Biarritz and Bordeaux, but these days he is very much a citizen of the Midi. That's how he came to learn that the municipality of the Var, and in particular the village of La Celle, was looking for tenders to resurrect a small hotel that in the nineteen-thirties had been owned and run by Sylvia Fournier, proprietor of the island of Porquerolles. Ducasse was familiar with the Var as one of the last unspoiled areas in the vicinity of the Côte d'Azur, and thus the possibility of another retreat in the mould of Moustiers suggested itself. The two establishments have a lot in common. Both are nestled in idyllic, Jean-de-Florette–type villages and both are in spectacular locations, one natural and the other architectural: Moustiers is at the foot of the Gorges du Verdon and the *hostellerie* in La Celle is adjacent to a twelfth-century Romanesque Benedictine abbey.

The village of La Celle is a couple of miles from Brignoles, the capital of central Vars. Its abbey makes an unusual and atmospheric backdrop to Ducasse's new laid-back retreat.

The restaurant is framed on one side by its rugged stone architecture and on the other by a wall of two-century-old cypress pines. Considering its history, it is not entirely inappropriate that immediately next door to the abbey there is an establishment devoted to life's pleasures: the Abbaye de la Celle was closed down in the seventeenth century because of the libertine behaviour of its resident nuns! Despite this historic sex scandal, the local council nonetheless turned out to be uncomfortable with the idea of allowing the adjacent eighteenth-century *hostellerie* to be used again for meeting and eating. Eventually Ducasse put his foot down and threatened to walk out on the whole deal. He won out, and so now the hotel that was popular with De Gaulle among others is back to the form it was in when Mme Fournier was at the helm.

The key word here is atmosphere. The locals play *pétanque* in the village square, the stone fountain is right next to it, and any minute you expect a creature like Manon to come skipping down the street with her goats. In short, this is exactly the type of place we hope to find in Provence. And thankfully it means you don't need to experience the whole Peter Mayle process of buying and renovating your own ruin to appreciate the character of the area.

The ten guest rooms of the *hostellerie* are far grander and more substantial than those at Moustiers, and are furnished with a selection of antiques that Ducasse has picked up through his travels in Provence and beyond. For the food – very much part of the Ducasse approach – he teamed up with another chef of the Midi, Bruno Clément, known for his culinary creations with truffles. The menu is simple and unpretentious, concentrating on variants of traditional local dishes. Because La Celle is less than an hour from Marseilles, fish is always available, and much of the produce comes from the kitchen gardens or the local markets. What's on offer is therefore always local, seasonal, and of the very highest quality.

---

address Hostellerie de l'Abbaye de la Celle, Place du Général de Gaulle, 83170 La Celle

telephone (33) 4 98 05 14 14 **fax** (33) 4 98 05 14 15

room rates from FF 1,250 (suites from FF 1,700)

les ateliers de l'image

St-Rémy is known as the heart of Provence, and for good reason. From here it's only thirty minutes to Avignon, less than an hour to Marseilles airport, an hour from Aix-en-Provence, forty minutes from the Pont du Gard and twenty minutes or so to Arles. But not only is St-Rémy geographically at the heart of Provence, this village is also its visual embodiment. From the architecture to the surrounding Alpille hills to the Wednesday vegetable market, it is without a doubt one of the prettiest villages in Provence. Once you get off the A7 autoroute (the infamous Route du Soleil) the country road that leads to St-Rémy is one of those oak tunnels so characteristic of France, an endless parade of regularly planted trees whose dense foliage provide a canopy of shade for the traveller. In times of stagecoach travel, these were a thoroughly welcome respite from the relentless heat of the southern sun. The other visual cliché straight from the cover of so many coffee table books on Provence are the endless fields of lavender, grown for the perfume industry.

The town of St-Rémy itself, arranged in a circle around its old walled centre, is packed with pretty stone houses with faded painted shutters and lined with cafés, brasseries and restaurants. For St-Rémy is a great place to eat. The average brasserie features local specialities such as rack of lamb and *escargots* and just about anything made with tomatoes.

All in all it's understandable that St-Rémy should be such a popular destination. Photographer Antoine Godard certainly thought so. He used to earn his living by organizing workshops and photography tours for American colleges that took in most of the sites of Provence. At that stage he was operating out of a hotel in Avignon. St-Rémy struck him as a much more appropriate base. The opportunity to put his plans into play came in the form of the town's dilapidated theatre and music hall. Once upon a time, Yves Montand and other chanteurs performed here. In fact, according to Godard, St-Rémy was something of a Nashville of the Midi, and the music hall was its Grand Old Oprey. Tucked into a lane in the heart of the village, it was the perfect location for what Godard had in mind – and the perfect space as well. The concept of an art hotel is now successfully established, but Godard wanted to be the first to do the same for photography. The gigantic building that used to be a 500-seat cinema and music hall is ideally suited to exhibitions of photography.

Tucked up a lane in the heart of old St-Rémy, Les Ateliers de l'Image is perfectly located but alas not easy to find

The main space of this former music hall converted by a photographer resembles a giant photographic studio

The only Provençal cliché here is the odd wall painted in terracotta or ochre

The full volume of the auditorium was given over to the central hotel space, used as bar, restaurant and lobby

Built on the top and sides of the old theatre, the rooms are unexpectedly light and spacious

The stage is still visible in the renovated structure. These days it is used for photography exhibitions

The hotel is also equipped with state-of-the art darkrooms and its workshops are operated in close association with with various American photography colleges. There is for example a one-week course which includes visits to all the most spectacular sites of Provence, followed by daily tutorials in developing and printing the results. As Godard says, if you love photography, it's important to experience, at least once in your life, the thrill of seeing an image appear on photographic paper.

That said, most people who stay in this three-star hotel are neither photographers nor photography buffs. They come here because it is such an unexpected surprise: an immense modern space in a quaint antique village. Even more surprisingly, despite its central location, it is surrounded by trees and hidden away at the end of a long leafy path. Hôtel Les Ateliers de l'Image has the ambience of a gigantic photographic studio, right down to the usual photographer's obsession with sound systems (not too many hotel lobbies benefit from the latest, most sophisticated Bang & Olufsen installation). Architecturally, the conversion of the theatre was highly successful. It preserves the original volume of the auditorium while also providing completely new guest rooms. The architect, who happens to be Godard's brother-in-law, retained the cinema space at the centre of the structure and either hung the rooms from the sides or literally placed them on top. Because of the irregular shape of the building, they are anything but your standard hotel rectangles. One of the best design features, however, are the large profile timber louvres mounted in steel frames which provide all the protection you could want from the Midi sun. There's also a small swimming pool in the front courtyard of the hotel, which is very popular with the guests. But architecture aside, the most irresistible feature of Les Ateliers de l'Image is the fact that when you walk the sixty-odd feet down the lane and turn right, you are immediately in the centre of old St-Rémy, the heart of Provence.

---

address Hôtel Les Ateliers de l'Image, 5 avenue Pasteur, 13210 St-Rémy-de-Provence

telephone (33) 4 90 92 51 50 **fax** (33) 4 90 92 43 52

room rates from FF 660

la bastide de moustiers

The ingredient is queen – or so rings the most quoted motto of French superchef Alain Ducasse. The only trouble is that amidst the lofty ceilings, fireplaces, walls of *trompe l'oeil* books, and fine Limoges and Courtauld linen of his restaurant in Paris, or the marble piers, gilded mirrors, golden silk and Louis XV chairs of his famed establishment in Monte Carlo, the humble claims of simplicity ring a little hollow. In his defence he is referring to his food not the decor, and even in his three-star establishments, Ducasse has made it clear that he is not interested in complexity. Many dishes in his repertoire consist of just two main ingredients plus one flavouring agent, and another Ducasse trademark is the use of one ingredient in several different ways in the same dish. Nonetheless, the cuisine, no matter how disciplined and pared down, cannot escape the fact that it is presented in the style traditionally recognized as '*le grand luxe à la française*'.

La Bastide de Moustiers was his opportunity to remedy all that. Set in a seventeenth-century *bastide* or fortified farmhouse near the famous village of Moustiers-Ste-Marie, some sixty miles inland from Aix-en-Provence, Ducasse was finally able to return to the very roots of his career as a chef – to his youth on his father's *foie gras* farm in Les Landes. Here in the relaxed setting of an utterly wild and unspoiled corner of Provence, Ducasse is able to send out Provençal fare – Sisteron lamb, Cavaillon medaillons, Banon cheese – without, as one journalist put it, 'the fuss and the feathers'.

In this idyllic hotel set in the shadows of the dramatic Gorges du Verdon, a maximum of thirty guests get to experience food the way Ducasse prefers it – and not just in the eating. At Bastide de Moustiers the ingredient is not just queen, it is part of the decor. Shiny purple aubergines and dusty red tomatoes roll down the corridors, crates of apples and figs are stacked by the door leading to the rear courtyard, and wrought-iron racks laden with cooling aromatic pastries surround the rear walls of the building. Wherever you look the ingredient is just behind you – and sometimes underneath your next step. Even the doors of both kitchens – one for pastry and one for entrées and main courses – are left open all the time. This is not just symbolic of the relaxed attitude of the place, but clearly intended to involve the audience. It's an introduction to the process as well as to the result.

It's a convincing approach, though maybe a sneaky one: for even if you are not hungry, you soon will be, and that surely is the point. It's almost like a primitive harvest dance intended to get the natives all excited about the feast they are about to consume. Above all it's a thoroughly original way to operate a small provincial inn. The experience of staying at La Bastide de Moustiers is not one you are likely to forget. Even today, almost two years after I first visited, I can remember very clearly what was on the menu for dinner one day and lunch the next.

Quite aside from Ducasse's back-to-basics experience, however, Moustiers-Ste-Marie, just up the road, is also an incredibly rewarding place to be between meals. This is one of the most photographed villages in all of France. Perhaps because of its precarious setting, Moustiers has escaped the onslaught of boutiques and banks that so often follows in the wake of tourism. And for the outdoor enthusiast this area is paradise. Unlike the more tame, almost suburban experience of Provence around cities like Aix and Marseilles, the Gorges du Verdon are a gateway to canoeing, hiking, whitewater rafting, caving, hang-gliding and rock-climbing. The nearest autoroute is miles away, the road through the countryside is single lane and most of the tourists are healthy fresh-faced French sportsmen and women who come to this area to confront the challenges of its rugged natural setting.

Ducasse's venture into the unspoiled *campagne* has made such an impact that once in a while the odd helicopter from Monaco makes a landing packed with aristocratic diners who want to see for themselves if dining without crystal chandeliers, mahogany panelling, wrought-iron staircases, a wine list of sixteen hundred-odd bottles, and fifty waiters really is as enjoyable as is claimed. Maybe, maybe not. In any case, for many it would be the first time in a long time that they have seen a fresh tomato.

---

address La Bastide de Moustiers, Chemin de Quinson, 04360 Moustiers-Ste-Marie

telephone (33) 4 92 70 47 47   **fax** (33) 4 92 70 47 48

room rates from FF 900 (suites from FF 1,550)

hôtel byblos

You can tell a lot about a place from the music they play in the morning. At Hôtel Byblos, it's Barry White.

If the makers of Ally McBeal were ever to contemplate a summer escape special, Byblos would be the perfect location. They certainly wouldn't have to employ extras; in fact they would hardly need to bring the cast. The guests at Byblos are good-looking, well-dressed and odd enough to stand in for them. This after all has been *the* place to stay in St-Tropez for the better part of three decades. Byblos is to St-Tropez what the Chateau Marmont is to Los Angeles – an institution for the stars, past and present.

Legend or not, many consider Byblos pretentious (which it is), overtly exhibitionistic (which it is), curiously dated (which it is) and far too expensive (which it is). Yet despite all these shortcomings, the allure of Hôtel Byblos endures. In a way the place is a paradox – a five-star hotel in a fishing village. Inside the compound it is a colourful, loose interpretation of traditional St-Tropez architecture with a distinct Arabic twist. It employs an army of fresh-faced staff who have been trained to deal with a clientele that, diverse as it may be, is consistently demanding. Plenty of valets are on hand to take care of the St-Tropez parking problem; legions of bus boys ensure the Louis Vuitton suitcases and Hermes bags make it to your room; and for those who have no intention of lifting a pinky once ensconced in a poolside recliner, a gaggle of waiters and waitresses serve the *salade niçoise* and *homard roti* to the luxuriously immobile.

Is it a decadent scene? Absolutely. How decadent? Consider that the hotel's famous nightclub, Les Caves du Roy, is the second largest single consumer of champagne in France. Not that the guests benefit in any way from bulk discount: a bottle of simple Dom will set you back hundreds of pounds, and a jeroboam of Crystal about two thousand. This is a place where the rich old man/beautiful young woman combination is the norm. Tasteless perhaps, but also irresistibly interesting. It's the Jack Nicholson phenomenon: you know the Byblos is bad, but in an increasingly politically correct world, that is the appeal. I'm not sure I'd want to spend an entire vacation here, but for a few days it certainly qualifies as a unique and fascinating experience. See and be seen is the name of the game. And to play it you need to take very seriously the matter of resort wardrobe. As a recent travel journalist

commented in an exasperated tone 'everyone, even the valets, has a "look".'

So the Byblos is flash, the clientele rich and the scene decadent bordering on sleazy. But what is it really like to stay here? Surprisingly relaxing, actually. Forbidden fruits aside, Hôtel Byblos couldn't have retained its status without also being a very good hotel. And as with St-Tropez itself, you decide how much of it you want to be part of. Its location, perched on a hill right in the heart of the old town, means you can if you wish avoid entirely the poolside scene by drinking at the quayside cafés. Or venture out through the old village square where the locals still play *boules* to check out some of St-Tropez's small and stylish boutiques.

The Arabic twist of the design is no accident. Opened in 1967, the hotel realized the dream of Lebanese property developer Jean-Prosper Gay Para of building a palace without rival in the Mediterranean. A *Thousand and One Nights* fantasy in a traditional fishing port: extravagant perhaps, but right from the very beginning this hotel achieved its aim of becoming a place where the international elite could find the luxury, sophistication and hedonism to which they aspired. In other words, it was to be a place where they could party. *La Légende* – Brigitte Bardot – attended the opening while on her honeymoon with German playboy industrialist Günter Sachs. Mick Jagger, Elton John and the rest have all had dinner in the coffered-ceilinged Lebanese room with its mother-of-pearl inlaid furniture. No doubt they have also danced on the tables amid the oriental decor of Les Caves du Roy.

With its sixties ceramics by Vallauris, Greek-inspired mosaics, a scattering of stone antiquities, and the tiled roofs and coloured facades traditional to St-Tropez, Byblos is as strange a mix as its customers. It will never win design awards, but it will also never be boring. For me, sitting poolside nursing a Campari and orange, the line from Peter Seller's film *Being There* kept coming to mind: 'I like to watch'.

address Hôtel Byblos, Avenue Paul Signac, 83990 St-Tropez
telephone (33) 4 94 56 68 00 **fax** (33) 4 94 56 68 01
room rates from FF 1,680 (suites from FF 3,600)

les moulins

St-Tropez, everyone will tell you, is a madhouse in the summer. Traffic into and out of this one-time fishing village is bumper to bumper and there is never anywhere to park. On a summer's day, it's not uncommon for the queues to start building up as far away as St-Maxine. From there it's a slow, hot crawl on the seaside road leading into the old port.

Still, the place is legendary. It is where Roger Vadim brought Brigitte Bardot to film *And God Created Woman*. By the nineteen-fifties it had already been an artists' colony for half a century. And today, despite the crowds, the traffic and the prices (almost as outrageous as the traffic), people still flock here every summer. They are the 'we will pay to play' crowd, plus all the people fascinated by them, who come to St-Tropez to gawk like we used to at the zoo, back when zoos were still exotic.

The big question people who don't know St-Tropez always ask is 'why?' Why put up with the cars, the queues and the expense when surely the whole scene is the opposite of the spirit of vacation? Why not just stay in a big city? On the surface it seems a valid protest, but the annual locals will insist that it's all a matter of choice. If you want the scene, it's there – if you want peace, sunshine and beautiful beaches, these are also easy to find. This combination of *la campagne* and *la vie jetset* is the key attraction of St-Tropez, and the reason there are countless vacation homes surrounding the old port. Most regulars choose a secluded escape in the nearby countryside – preferably a renovated farmhouse surrounded by olive trees and plenty of dense green around the swimming pool for privacy. Then when they are in the mood, they head down to the Vieux Port for some shopping and people-watching from under the red awnings of the legendary Café Sénéquier.

St-Tropez is one of the most popular places in France for villa vacations. Parisian paediatricians, Swedish stockbrokers, British bankers and Dutch dentists form an international community of high-incomers who regularly return here to stay in their own or a rented villa. Seclusion as the rule, action when you want it: this is the mix that makes St-Tropez.

Until recently it was a mix largely reserved for the villa crowd. But not everyone can justify the price of a small car for a week of the St-Tropez lifestyle, and for many the prospect of sharing a house for a week or two (which is how most villa tenants spread the cost) is more

punishment than reward. That's where Les Moulins enters the picture. Situated on the outskirts of St-Tropez, on the way to the famous Pampelonne beach, Les Moulins is a converted farmhouse surrounded by a splendid garden. It has retained all its rugged charm, and the interiors are exactly what you would expect from Brigitte Bardot's stamping ground. While the exterior is all green, ivy-clad and rustic, the interiors are crisp, whitewashed and romantic. Lots of linen, lots of voile, plenty of pillows and plenty of white-tiled surfaces combine to create a perfect south of France magazine fantasy.

But attractive as they are, the rooms are not the main appeal of Les Moulins; that is its seclusion. After the hurly burly of the old port, and the out-and-out exhibitionism on the beach, Les Moulins is a quiet and pretty retreat from all the madness. It has major advantages over a villa: you don't have to make your own bed, work in the garden, clean the pool (there isn't one), or make coffee for a small army in the morning, and you don't have to be nice to house guests who didn't take the hint last year. There's also the major plus of Les Moulins' kitchen. The proprietor Christophe Leroy made his name with great restaurants in St-Tropez, and Les Moulins has followed suit by becoming a dinner destination in its own right. Every night the restaurant is booked out – a problem for outsiders but a reassuring statistic for hotel guests, for it means that on the odd night that you don't feel like going out, you have the advantage of one of the better restaurants of St-Tropez as your in-house kitchen.

Now back to the traffic. In the summer, St-Tropez is nothing if not predictable. After everyone has struggled at a slow crawl to get into the centre of town in the morning, the next guaranteed mass destination is *la plage*. In this you are ahead of the game because Les Moulins is on the road to the beaches. You can be there long before the spectacle starts – although most regulars would wonder why you might want to do that.

address Les Moulins, Route des Plages, 83350 Ramatuelle

telephone (33) 4 94 97 17 22   **fax** (33) 4 94 97 72 70

room rates from FF 1,250 (suites from FF 1,450)

le mélézin

Sooner or later, even the most die-hard chalet junkie needs a break from a visual diet of cowbells, antlers and old wood. There is a generous handful of hotels in the French Alps catering superbly to traditional expectations, but when it comes to finding an alternative style vision, particularly a modern one, it's difficult to imagine what that should be. I know of the odd hotel in the purpose-built resorts like Tignes that has kept its original 'funky' sixties interior, but somehow beaten-up orange plastic furniture and chocolate-brown shag-pile carpet on the walls as well as the floor is not the alternative I have in mind. The only Alpine hotel I know that has successfully created a beautiful interior without resorting to mountain clichés is Le Mélézin in Courchevel.

If Yves Saint Laurent had been a skier, then his chalet would probably look like this. Le Mélézin is distinctly more exotic and oriental than most hotels in the snow. Paris-based architect Ed Tuttle, who also designed the very successful and very sexy Amankila, Amanjiwo, Amangani, Amanpuri and Amanjena used a palette of materials that are well suited to a place in the snow – but suited in a way quite unlike what we are used to. The walls in the dining room, the library, and the bar, for

example, are panelled in oak in a grid-like design that looks like a modern interpretation of Tudor. Inset into this grid are panels of weathered black leather or hand-blown reflective glass. Combined with floors of dark, polished timber and deep-grey cotton carpet, the effect is simple but sumptuous. In the guest rooms the approach is altogether different. Here Tuttle has opted for pale, serene neutrals: cedar bedheads and sliding panels that screen the large expanses of glass at night, light-grey granite stone in the open-plan bathrooms, and neutral silks, cottons and linens that blend into a softly monochrome and multi-textured scheme.

Le Mélézin suits Courchevel very well. Together with Méribel and Val Thorens, this resort is promoted collectively as Les Trois Vallées, the largest ski-able terrain in the world. There are other resorts in France that refute this claim, but it is undeniable that in the Trois Vallées the French have developed a ski resort that is almost unimaginably vast. In a single uninterrupted day of flat-out skiing you would be lucky to cover every piste that belongs just to Courchevel, let alone the other two mountains. Courchevel was specifically designed to take skiing to a new level, and in

its facilities it does just that. Its altitude makes it 'snow safe', and because it was purpose built, practicalities such as car parking and the like have all been planned very well. The inevitable downside is that it lacks the authenticity and ambience of a real village. There are no farmhouses or churches here. At an altitude of 1,850 metres, Courchevel is above the tree line – no village would ever have been built so high up. Everything was created specifically for ski tourism.

Here more than anywhere was a place to abandon all the Alpine clichés. With Le Mélézin the Aman group created something exciting and different, like Courchevel itself. But innovation *per se* was not the goal – luxury was. Under the direction of Aman guru Adrian Zecha, the group set out to build a winter equivalent of the sensual and indulgent hotels in tropical Asia with which it made its name. The rooms at Le Mélézin are typically four times the size of those of more traditional chalets, as are the bathrooms. They all open onto balconies or terraces, and they all have views of the mountains. In fact the hotel is literally on the slopes, jutting boldly – almost arrogantly – onto one of the pistes. Then there's the health centre. The steam room is vintage Aman – a monumental structure in a very pale local limestone, unquestionably the most beautiful hammam I've ever seen. The infinitely attentive approach continues on the timber decks of the hotel, where each wooden chair is draped with a folded Scottish plaid blanket. In fine weather these decks serve as an extension of the hotel's public spaces, making a great location for an early coffee, late breakfast or lunch.

When it comes to skiing, Le Mélézin does everything for you. Instructors collect you from the hotel, reception organizes your ski pass, and the ski room is equipped with a state-of-the-art boot drying machine that not only dries the boots but neutralizes their odour. No more smelly ski boots – that's surely the ultimate in Alpine luxury.

address Le Mélézin, Rue Bellecote, 73120 Courchevel
telephone (33) 4 79 08 01 33   **fax** (33) 4 79 08 08 96
room rates from FF 2,600 (suites from FF 7,500)

trianon palace

For anyone planning to visit Versailles, there is no more appropriate place to stay than the Trianon Palace. Versailles was the crowning achievement of the Sun King, Louis XIV. The gardens he created with André Le Nôtre are the world's most magnificent and enduring example of man's will imposed over nature. The fact that this spectacle was achieved three centuries ago makes it even more impressive today. Equally majestic are the extravagant baroque interiors of the King's Palace at Versailles, a huge glittering monument filled with unimaginable treasures, all to show the world the glory and superiority of France.

After a day of being engrossed in an environment that would leave even the most blasé person in awe, returning to a cosy, charming little hotel is unthinkable. Versailles puts you in the mood for grandeur, and that's exactly what the Trianon Palace provides.

Built in 1910 on the site of a former Capuchin friary right on the edge of Le Nôtre's gardens, this splendid building with its classical facade has an eventful history of its own. In 1919 the final stages of the treaty of Versailles were negotiated here in the famous Salon Clemenceau, named after the French president Georges Clemenceau who presented the conditions of the treaty to the Germans. During the war the hotel had been the headquarters of the Allied War Committee, but afterwards the Trianon Palace resumed its role as a favourite retreat for the rich and famous. It was frequented by figures from the theatrical and literary worlds — including the likes of Marcel Proust, Sarah Bernhardt, Colette, Sacha Guitry and Yvonne Printemps. Business tycoons too, like J. Paul Getty, André Citroën and John D. Rockefeller, crossed paths in the hotel's imposing gallery. Even the Duke and Duchess of Windsor were recorded as guests when they spent part of their honeymoon in the palace.

But in 1939 the hotel was again requisitioned for wartime use, first by Britain's Royal Air Force, and then, after the German occupation, by the Luftwaffe. Goering had quite a taste for the finer things in life, so it's no surprise that he decided to make his home amidst the marble, mirror and crystal of this splendid building. After the Liberation, the military musical chairs continued when the Trianon Palace became the headquarters of the American forces. But when the likes of Eisenhower, Patton and Marshall eventually departed, the usual crowd returned: King Hussein, the Aga Khan, Queen Elizabeth II,

King Ibn Saud … though the presence of all of them was overshadowed by the scandal created by Marlene Dietrich in 1947, when she sparked international headlines by turning up for dinner wearing trousers.

Today the roll-call of celebrities continues unabated. Tom Cruise, Jessica Lange, John Travolta, Jacques Brel, Arthur Rubinstein – the spectacular beauty of the surroundings and the grandeur of the Trianon Palace make, it seems, a combination too seductive to resist. And although only twenty minutes from Paris by car, Versailles is not just beautiful but quiet. The French government, to its credit, decided to route the major motorways far enough from Louis XIV's masterpiece so as not to disturb the peace of the public parks.

This democratic gesture, interestingly, has an historical precedent. Contrary to what people might expect of one of history's largest egos, the Sun King's gardens were always open to the public … provided you had a hat and sword (so no women, I presume). Even this,

however, was not as elitist as it might sound since both hat and sword were available for hire at the gate.

The attractions of Versailles are clear, but this being France, food must also rate a mention. The restaurant at the Trianon Palace, Les Trois Marches, has had two Michelin stars since 1976, so it's something of an institution. And even the Café Trianon enjoys the talents of Benoit Rambaud, who has been *chef de cuisine* for the better part of a decade.

In 1991, a 28,000 square foot spa facility was added to this grand hotel known affectionately as the great white wedding cake. This addition presented one potential aesthetic downside – all those guests in bathrobes and fluffy slippers making their unsightly way down chandelier-bedecked corridors. The hotel, to its credit, seems to have anticipated this horror, for it installed a series of hidden lifts and corridors that allow you to go back and forth between the pool and your room without being spotted in public.

---

address Trianon Palace, 1 boulevard de la Reine, 78000 Versailles

telephone (33) 1 30 84 38 00 **fax** (33) 1 30 84 50 01

room rates from FF 2,800 (suites from FF 3,500)

© 2001 Herbert Ypma

First published in paperback in the United States of
America in 2001 by Thames & Hudson Inc.,
500 Fifth Avenue, New York, New York 10110

Library of Congress Catalog Card Number 00-108869
ISBN 0-500-28268-4

Designed by Maggi Smith

Printed and bound in Singapore by CS Graphics